Urban Structure
and Victimization

Urban Structure and Victimization

David L. Decker
David Shichor
California State College,
  San Bernardino
Robert M. O'Brien
University of Oregon

LexingtonBooks
D.C. Heath and Company
Lexington, Massachusetts
Toronto

Library of Congress Cataloging in Publication Data

Decker, David L.
  Urban structure and victimization.

  Bibliography: p.
  Includes index.
  1. Victims of crime—United States. 2. Victims of crimes surveys—United
States. 3. Aged—United States—Crimes against. 4. City and town life—
United States. I. Shichor, David. II. O'Brien, Robert M. III. Title.
HV6783.D43   362.8′8   79-1865
ISBN 0-669-02951-3   AACR2

Published simultaneously in Canada

Printed in the United States of America

International Standard Book Number: 0-669-02951-3

Library of Congress Catalog Card Number: 79-1865

Contents

Tables		ix
Preface and Acknowledgments		xi
Chapter 1	**Studying the Victims of Crime**	1
	Criminal Victimization	1
	The Status of Victims in the Past	2
	The Study of the Victim	4
	Victimization of Organizations	9
	The Future Use of Victim Studies	10
Chapter 2	**Urban Structural Analysis**	13
	Human Ecology and Crime	13
	Some Methodological Issues	18
	Sampled Cities: A Limitation	19
Chapter 3	**Victimization Surveys: A Comparison of Reported Crime Rates and Victimization Rates**	21
	Uniform Crime Reports and National Crime Surveys	21
	Absolute Differences in UCR and NCS Estimated Crime Rates	24
	An Empirical Assessment of the Validity of NCS and UCR Rates	25
	Procedures	27
	Findings	30
	Discussion	32
	Summary	33
Chapter 4	**An Empirical Classification of Criminal Victimization**	37
	Discovering a Classification for Crimes	38
	Some Applications of the Empirical Classification	40
	Summary	42

Chapter 5   **Population Density, Crowding, and Criminal**
                   Victimization   45

                   Previous Studies of Population Density and
                       Crowding   46
                   Studies of Variations in Intercity Crime Rates   47
                   Procedures   49
                   Findings   50
                   Discussion   52

Chapter 6   **Law-Enforcement Manpower and Criminal**
                   Victimization   55

                   Procedures   57
                   Findings   57
                   Discussion   58
                   Summary   62

Chapter 7   **Patterns of Juvenile Victimization**   65

                   Procedures   66
                   Findings   66
                   Discussion   70
                   Summary   71

Chapter 8   **Household Victimization of the Elderly**   73

                   Procedures   75
                   Findings   76
                   Summary   78

Chapter 9   **Research and Social-Policy Implications**   79

                   Validity of UCR and NCS Data   79
                   Classification of Crimes   79
                   Density and Crowding   80
                   Limitations Resulting from Sample Size   80
                   Social-Policy Implications   81

Appendix A   **NCS Survey Design**   83

Appendix B   **Definitions of Crimes Used in the NCS and the**
                   UCR   85

Appendix C   **NCS and UCR Rates and Structural**
                   Characteristics of Twenty-six Central Cities   89

Contents

Bibliography   95

Index   109

About the Authors   115

Tables

3-1	Differences in the Mean Rates Based on UCR and NCS Estimates for Twenty-six Cities	24
3-2	Correlations between the Structural Characteristics of Twenty-six Central Cities	29
3-3	Correlation between Victimization and UCR Rates for Various Types of Crimes in Twenty-six Cities	30
3-4	Correlation of UCR and NCS Rates with Important Structural Characteristics of Twenty-six Cities	31
4-1	Zero-Order Correlations between Structural Characteristics of Cities and Ten Types of Crime	39
4-2	Typology of Criminal Victimization	40
4-3	Comparison of Correlations between Population Density and Crimes Combined According to the UCR Classification and the Grounded Typology	41
5-1	Zero-Order Correlations between Internal and External Density and Victimization Rates	50
5-2	Proportions of Intercity Variations in Victimization Rates Accounted For by Internal and External Density	51
6-1	Zero-Order Correlations between the Number of Police per Capita, Population Density, and Ten Types of Offenses	59
6-2	Partial Correlations between the Number of Police per Capita, Population Density, and Ten Types of Offenses	60
7-1	Stepwise Regression for Property Crimes without Contact	67
7-2	Stepwise Regression for Nonproperty Assaultive Crimes	69
8-1	Victimizations Reported on the NCS and Classified as Household Victimizations, by Age Groups	75
8-2	Stepwise Regression for Household Burglary of the Elderly, Regressed on Structural Characteristics of Central Cities	76

8-3   Stepwise Regression for Household Larceny of the
           Elderly, Regressed on Structural Characteristics of
           Central Cities   77

Preface and Acknowledgments

The idea for this book grew out of a series of collaborative studies by the authors, using victimization rates from National Crime Surveys in twenty-six central cities of the United States. The research reported in this book follows the human-ecological tradition of criminological inquiry, the brief history of which is reviewed in chapter 2, and the data used are on the city level of analysis.

Chapter 3 provides a comparison of the validity of crime rates based on the Uniform Crime Reports and those used throughout this book (from the National Crime Surveys). Our first major discovery in using these data was that, contrary to professional opinion, a positive relationship was *not* found between the population density of cities (population per square mile) and victimization rates for all types of crime (see chapter 5). We then discovered a distinct pattern to the relationships between specific types of crime (property crimes without contact, property crimes with contact, and nonproperty assaultive crimes), and the major structural characteristics of these cities (chapter 4). In chapter 6, we examine the relationship of victimization rates to population density and the number of police per capita, and, in chapter 7 we look at the patterns of juvenile victimization. In chapter 8, we examine the relationship between the structural characteristics of cities and household victimization rates for the elderly.

This book is designed as a resource book for college instructors, researchers, and upper-level undergraduate or graduate students of criminology, urban sociology, and human ecology. It also should be of interest to those involved in the policy sciences.

In writing this book, we have incurred several debts. We would like to thank the staff of the computer center at California State College, San Bernardino, for their help; Jane Rowland and Mary Schmidt for typing the manuscript; and the staff at Lexington Books for their prodding to finish the book and their aid in preparing it. Since the authors worked collaboratively over a number of years and contributed equally to the project, the order of authorship was determined by a flip of a coin.

Studying the Victims of Crime

Victimology—the study of victims—became an established field of study during the 1960s and 1970s. The growth of professional interest in this field is reflected in the large number of books and articles written; the establishment of a specialized journal, *Victimology*; the organization of international conferences (the first in Jerusalem in 1973); and the creation of agencies designed to assist victims, such as the National Organization of Victim Assistance (NOVA). In addition, several national and international workshops on victimology have been organized, and the World Society of Victimology was established in 1980.

The term *victimology* was coined by Benjamin Mendelsohn (1963), who envisioned victimology not as a subfield of criminology but as a separate field of study. Victimology was intended to study victims in the most comprehensive manner. Accordingly Mendelsohn (1975) developed the concept of "victimity," which he characterized as the "whole of the socio-bio-psychological characteristics, common to all victims in general, which society wishes to prevent and fight, no matter what their determinants are (criminals or others)" (p. 25). Dadrian (1976), another proponent of this general approach to the study of victims, viewed victimology as "the study of the social processes through which individuals and groups are maltreated in such a way that social problems are created" (p. 40).

Although this general approach to victimology has been followed by some people, the mainstream of victimological work and thought concentrates on the victims of crimes. The majority of researchers currently studying victimology draw a clear connection between criminology and victimology, and their major focus is analysis of the relationship between the victim and the criminal.

Criminal Victimization

The term *victim* not only is descriptive but also carries certain underlying assumptions. Ziegenhagen (1977) notes that there usually is an implication that the victim is innocent and therefore has a moral claim for compassion and sympathy from others. Victims are often considered to be almost passive recipients of the actions affecting them. It is interesting, however, that many legal scholars do not include the victim among the essential com-

1

ponents of criminal law, whereas the role of the state, the form of retribution against the offender, psychological and behavioral specifications concerning criminal acts, and juristic standards are specified in detail. Although the concept of the victim is not clearly included in the law, however, the various components of the law do have important implications for the victim. The representatives of the state determine which law violations are to be punished, and selective enforcement of laws is in the hands of these representatives (for example, antitrust violations often are not enforced, even though antitrust laws were designed to protect the interests of the victims). Similarly, retributive penal sanctions, which might provide some satisfaction to many victims, are administered in a highly selective manner.

Whatever the reasons for these policies and practices (rehabilitation, problems of evidence, allocation of criminal-justice resources, and so forth), they do not necessarily take the victim's point of view into consideration. Even the punishment component of the law is often applied "as a tool to influence the future behavior of the lawbreaker rather than as a device providing satisfaction for those individuals who are harmed through violation of the law" (Ziegenhagen 1977, p. 3). The major emphasis is on establishing the intent (mens rea) of the criminal; when the victim is considered in this context, it is to determine the criminal's responsibility—that is, what the victim's contribution was to the commitment of the crime (such as in justifiable homicide).

The Status of Victims in the Past

In a historical review, Schafer (1977) explores the role of the victim in the past. He notes that, in ancient times, social control was in the hands of individuals. Because of insufficient social organization, people were forced to take the law into their own hands. The individual "made the law, and he was the victim, the prosecutor, and the judge" (Schafer 1977, p. 7). He revenged wrongdoings against himself and demanded compensation for himself.

When people began to live in larger groups, social control was maintained by the kindred group, and an offense against the individual was considered to be against the entire group. The individual victim's position became generalized to his extended family, and the offender enjoyed his family's backing. Thus, the matter of offense and victimization no longer was an interpersonal matter but had become an issue that had to be settled between two family groups. This development served as the basis for the concept of collective responsibility.

This arrangement of collective responsibility and blood feud resulted in a chain of endless violence, however, and people slowly realized that, rather than solving and terminating conflicts, it aggravated and prolonged them. In addition, it did not bring any tangible help to the injured party. The social arrangement of blood-revenge was a necessary device for ensuring the individual's survival, however, reflecting the fact that the major threat for the individual came from out-of-family sources, because problems within the family unit were controlled by the family members. The blood feud increased the cohesion of the family and served as a social defense against outsiders.

With the development of more stable economic systems and a higher level of material culture, the arrangement of compensation emerged. The historic beginnings of compensation can be found in various ancient sources. Probably the first known legal record in which compensation is mentioned is the Code of Hammurabi, which is probably known better as the source of retributive justice than of compensation. It very clearly outlines arrangements for compensation, when it states, for example:

> If the brigand has not been taken, the man plundered shall claim before God what he has lost; and the city and sheriff in whose land and boundary the theft has taken place shall restore to him all that he has lost. If a life, the city and sheriff shall pay one mina of silver to his people. (Edwards 1971, p. 31)

Ancient law is more a law of torts (civil law) than a law of crimes (Maine 1887), which means that almost all offenses that modern societies consider criminal violations—such as theft, robbery, assault, trespassing, and libel—were handled as torts in Roman law (Meiners 1978). Similarly, "the laws of primitive societies contained monetary evaluations for most offenses as compensation to the victims, not as a punishment of the criminal" (Laster 1975, p. 20).

In his exploration of the criminal-victim relationship among the ancient Germans, Tacitus stated:

> Even homicide is atoned by a certain fine in cattle and sheep; and the whole family accepts the satisfaction to the advantage of the public weal, since quarrels are most dangerous in a free state. (Schafer 1977, p. 11)

Crimes that resulted in social punishment in primitive law and in early Anglo-Saxon law were mainly sins—offenses against the deity (such as incest, witchcraft, and bestiality)—since these kinds of offenses could not be restituted to a single person or family (Laster 1975; Diamond 1935). During these periods, the victim was a major focus of interest in the law. The victim's role in the offense was not questioned; he was assumed to be innocent and passive, and his major role in the proceedings was to be compensated for the injury accrued. Thus, a basic reciprocity was built into the law.

Although, in these earlier periods, the seriousness of a crime was determined not only by the harm caused by the offense but also by the social status of the victim, the importance of the victim started to decline with the rising political and economic power of the kingship, on the one hand, and the Roman Catholic church, on the other. These two major political powers developed the concept of criminal law that considers most offenses committed by one individual against another as offenses against the state. Thus, the offender became responsible to the state (or the Crown) rather than to the individual. The victim's relation to the crime was viewed as a civil rather than a criminal matter and he could find remedies only through civil procedures. These developments clearly indicate the "decline of the victim" (Schafer 1977).

Toward the end of the nineteenth century, interest in the fate of the victim started to rise again. It again became evident that the violator of the criminal law usually causes not only social harm but personal harm. "There has been renewed recognition during the past few decades that crime gives rise to legal, moral, ethical, and psychic ties not only between the violator and society, but also between the violator and his victim" (Schafer 1977, p. 24). Thus, the relationship and interaction between the criminal and his victim again became a focus of study.

The Study of the Victim

Victim Classifications

Interest in the victims of crime reemerged mainly with efforts to understand the etiology of crime. As mentioned earlier, the general assumption had been that the victim's role in a criminal encounter was passive. Mendelsohn (1963), one of the pioneers of modern victimology, notes that he started his inquiry into the victim's role during the 1930s when, as a practicing lawyer, he wanted to know the "truth" about the criminal cases he handled. Since he was interested in the total crime situation, it became important to examine whether the victim contributed to the criminal act in any way.

Von Hentig (1948), another early researcher in victimology, focused on the victim's role. His point of view is expressed in the following statement:

> In a sense the victim shapes and molds the criminal. The poor and ignorant immigrant has bred a peculiar kind of fraud. Depressions and wars are responsible for new forms of crimes because new types of potential victims are brought into being. (p. 384)

This is a claim that certain types of people are predisposed to become victims. In this respect, Reckless (1973) separates two types of victims—one type classified by personal or social attributes, the other by behavior. He states:

> Certain categories of persons, property, and valuables seem to attract doer behavior because of their weaknesses or availability, while other kinds of individuals (property and valuables are not included here) appear to instigate criminal deeds in the doer as a result of escalation in social interaction, such as an exchange of insults, jealous accusations, unjustified obstruction, and so forth. (Reckless 1973, p. 91)

Several published studies deal with the first type of victim. A psychiatrist, Henri Ellenberger (1954), uses the term *victimogenesis*—meaning factors that predispose certain individuals to become victims. Among these predisposing factors, Von Hentig (1948) mentions being young, being female, being old, being mentally defective or deranged, being intoxicated, being an immigrant, being a member of a minority group, and having dull-normal intelligence. People in these categories have certain weaknesses that make them easier prey. He also examined the psychological aspects of victimogenesis and suggested the following psychological types as likely victims: the depressed or apathetic, the acquisitive or greedy, the wanton or sensual, the lonesome and heartbroken, the tormentor, and the blocked— "an individual who has been so enmeshed in a losing situation that defensive moves have become impossible or more injurious than the injury at criminal hands" (Von Hentig 1948, p. 433).

The victim's behavior as a contributing factor to the criminal act also has been examined by several contemporary social scientists. Wolfgang (1958) discusses victim-precipitated homicide as one in which physical force was first used by the victim. Amir (1971) also uses this concept in his research on forcible rape, and Normandeau (1968) uses it in property-crime victimization research.

There have been additional attempts to construct victim typologies that include both the personal attributes of the victim and behavioral factors. Fattah (1967), for example, suggests five major types of victims: (1) nonparticipating victims; (2) latent or predisposed victims—that is, those who have certain character predispositions to be victimized; (3) provocative victims; (4) participating victims; and (5) false victims, who either are not victims at all or victimize themselves. Sellin and Wolfgang (1964) suggest a typology of victimization rather than of victims: (1) primary victimization, referring to individual victims; (2) secondary victimization, referring to impersonal victims (such as organizations); (3) tertiary victimization, which involves the public or society; (4) mutual victimization, which refers to victims who themselves are offenders in a consensual act (such as adultery); and (5) no victimization, in which there is no recognizable victim. Galaway and Hudson (1981) propose a typology of victims based on the victim's responsibility for the crime: (1) unrelated victims, "who have no relationship whatsoever with their criminal"; (2) provocative victims, "who have done something against the offender"; (3) precipitative victims, "who have done nothing specifically against the criminal, but whose thoughtless behavior instigates, tempts, or allures the offender to commit a crime against the enticing victim"; (4) biologically weak victims, "whose constitution or physical or mental characteristics develop in the offender the idea of crime against them"; (5) socially weak victims, "who are usually not regarded by the larger society as fullfledged members of the community" (immigrants, ethnic minorities, and the like); (6) self-victimizing victims; and (7) political victims, "who suffer at the hands of their political opponents" (Galaway and Hudson 1981, pp. 22-23).

The Victim and the Criminal-Justice System

Several scholars studying victimization also point out that the criminal-justice system acts differently in accordance with the identity of the victim. Historically, the identities of both the offender and the victim have been determining factors in the administration of justice (Pritchard 1955; Barnes and Teeters 1959). To a degree, this is still true today, although in an informal way. Newman (1966), for example, found that the behavior and characteristics of the victim are important in the consideration of whether or not an offender is convicted. Williams (1976) also dealt with the relationship between victim characteristics and whether or not the defendant is found guilty. He found that, although victim characteristics affect the case-processing decisions in cases of violent crime (that is, the prosecutor's decisions to screen or continue a case), they did not appear to affect whether the defendant was found guilty or not guilty. The only factor that had an effect was the existence of a personal relationship between the victim and the defendant. The likelihood that a case will be dismissed or dropped (except in homicide cases) when there is a familial or friendship relation between the victim and the defendant is much higher than under other circumstances.

    In another study, Denno and Cramer (1976) concluded that "victim precipitation and the impression projected by the victim appear to be of significance to the judge in the sentencing process (p. 224). They mention that dress and general demeanor of the victim were reported as important, but ascribed factors, such as sex, age, and race, might have an even greater effect. These factors probably are not mentioned, however, because it would be legally unacceptable.

    The victim's importance at the trial stage of the criminal-justice process is well demonstrated through the proliferation of victim-witness programs. These programs were established because it became evident that the criminal-justice system pays a disproportionately large amount of attention to the offenders, protecting their rights and providing opportunities for their rehabilitation, while victims receive much less attention. If the offender is apprehended, the victim, as a witness, is subject to further inconveniences. Victims may have to appear several times in the courtroom, sacrificing time from work and submitting themselves to rigorous questioning on the witness stand. Therefore, victims often do not report the crimes or do not lodge complaints. This situation prompted the establishment of victim-witness programs that are designed to:

(1) . . . enhance the quality of justice by satisfying the emotional and social needs of crime victims and witnesses, and

(2) . . . increase the willingness of victims and witnesses to cooperate with police and prosecutors after they have reported a crime. (Rosenblum and Blew 1979, p. 3)

The programs concentrate on providing services in the following fields:

1. Public education—to provide citizens with information concerning crime prevention and the availability of victims services
2. Victim counseling—to handle emotional and social service needs of the individual
3. Witness services—to improve victim and witness participation in the criminal-justice process by providing practical information about how and when to come to the court and by providing such services as child care, transportation, and waiting rooms
4. Financial renumeration—such as compensation restitution and return of property (Rosenblum and Blew 1979).

Victim-witness assistance programs also are meant to increase the victim-witnesses' feelings that they are important participants in the criminal-justice procedures. As Knudten and Knudten (1981) point out:

As long as the victim and witness are treated as intervening actors and not as persons in need within the system, they will respond negatively. Only when these individuals perceive that their concerns are given equal attention to those related to the offender will they recognize that the system cares about them and values their participation. (p. 61)

The upsurge of interest in the victim and the studies in victimology have resulted in policy-oriented programs for victim compensation and in victim-restitution programs. Victim compensation provides public funds to victims of violent crimes or to their relatives (Edelhertz and Geis 1974). Compensation programs with various scopes of benefits and limitations have been established in several foreign countries and in several states of the United States (Harland 1981; Lamborn 1981).

Restitution, in contrast, is payment by the offender to the victims of crime "made within the jurisdiction of the criminal justice system" (Galaway and Hudson, 1975, p. 256). It is concerned not only with the renumeration to the victim, but also with bringing about

> better feelings in citizens about the quality of justice in their country; it may prove of value to victims; and it may help criminals to appreciate the nature of the harm they inflict on others. It may also serve to alleviate offender's alienation from a law-abiding existence. (Geis 1977, p. 162)

These ideas prompted the wide-scale development of various additional victim-assistance programs, such as counseling and emergency services, hotlines, victim advocacy—aimed at protecting the rights and interests of the victim during legal proceeding—and crime-prevention programs for the protection of prior victims of crime (Schneider and Schneider 1981).

The victim's role in the criminal-justice process at the police level also has been mentioned by Sellin and Wolfgang (1964), who found in their research that the attitude of the victim toward the delinquent or the delinquent act played an important role in police decision making. In fact, this factor was ranked in importance immediately after the prior record of the delinquent and the type of offense as one of the major factors in making a decision at the police level.

In a different vein, Wolfgang (1979) suggests that victim attributes and characteristics should be taken into consideration not only in scientific research but also in the formal criminal-justice process (for example, in adjudication and sentencing). He contends that sentencing should be based not only on the legal culpability of the offender but also on the degree of harm caused to a particular victim. This would bring about the individualization of the victim.

> If varying the attributes of the victim and consequences to the victim alters the degree of harm, corresponding variations in the penalty can be justifiably argued, so long as degrees of harm define seriousness and seriousness commands the sanction. (Wolfgang 1979, p. 22)

This issue is important and controversial. In ancient law, the social statuses of the offender and the victim were considered in deciding on a punishment. Since noblemen were more valuable under the law, for example, their victimization was considered a more serious offense.

Victimization of Organizations

Organizations are often easy victims of crime, because many people interact with them (such as officers, employees, suppliers, customers, and clients). Smigel and Ross (1970) point out that most of these people do not have much interest in the welfare of the organization, because they believe that large organizations are impersonal, that they emphasize means, that they are capable of absorbing losses, and so on. Organizations are vulnerable to crimes that have low visibility, such as employee theft, embezzlement, and bribery. Because of their unpopularity, the low-visibility crimes against them, and the public's lack of identification with them, organizations are "denied access to an important source of protection afforded the personal victim: the sympathy and conscience of the general population" (Smigel and Ross 1970, p. 5). In addition, the belief that organizations will be reimbursed by insurance further decreases public sympathy toward them as victims.

An interesting offshoot of the study of organizations as victims is the work of Dynes and Quarantelli (1974), concerning organizations as victims in mass civil disturbances. In their research, they examined the urban disorders of the 1960s and found that most of the damage in these disturbances focused on small retail-business establishments. According to their findings, these establishments were victimized (looted or burned) when they were closed—that is, not as a result of immediate confrontation. Dynes and Quarantelli (1974) reject the suggestion that these establishments might have been targeted as a retaliation for economic exploitation, as was outlined in *The Poor Pay More* (Caplovitz 1963). They mention the importance of the "collective definitions about 'imagined' economic exploitation," which might determine which businesses will have the higher risk of victimization (Dynes and Quarantelli 1974, p. 72). These definitions can change quickly, especially when higher values enter the situation, as, for example, when an emergency arises—such as someone being seriously injured or a fire getting out of control.

In mass-violence situations, the police are also a target, since they are identified as symbols of political exploitation. The police often become the major target for sniping; firefighters also can become victims, but the attitude toward them tends to be less hostile than the attitude toward the police. Nevertheless, the majority of deaths in mass civil disturbances were found to be ghetto residents.

Dynes and Quarantelli conclude that "the major organizational victims in civil disturbances are retail stores and the symbols of authority." The victimity of these targets seems to relate to the fact that they are the key contacts between the ghetto and the surrounding white society:

Retail stores and the police serve as the victims, less because of particular
discriminatory or repressive behavior on their part, but more because they
symbolize for the ghetto residents their comparative and enduring depriva-
tions. (Dynes and Quarantelli 1974, p. 74)

Within the last decade, criminal-victimization studies have become
more varied, including studies of special populations such as the elderly
(Goldsmith and Goldsmith 1976; Young Rifai 1977; Cook 1976; Sengstock
and Liang 1979; Furstenberg 1971), treatment of the victim by the criminal-
justice system (McDonald 1976), consequences for a wrongfully accused
person (Shichor 1975) or for the bystander (Sheleff and Shichor 1980; Pecar
1972; Sheleff 1974), victimization in correctional institutions (Bartolla,
Miller, and Dinitz 1976), victimization by the police (Binder and Scharf
1980), and victimization of the police by others (Lindsey 1980).

Finally, there have been attempts to ascertain the impact of victimological thinking and research on the shaping of the criminal law. Lamborn (1980) summarizes these changes in the law succinctly:

Both substance and procedure have been affected, with changes being
made by legislatures, courts, and administrative agencies. New crimes have
been created and definitions of old crimes have been modified; procedures
affecting both criminals and victims have been amended; and sentencing
practices and options have been changed. (p. 14)

The Future Use of Victim Studies

Wolfgang and Singer (1978) attempt to outline some areas in which victimization data may be useful in adding to the understanding of the
dynamics of crime. They mention corporate victimization as one of the
areas that can benefit from victimization surveys. By developing corporate
or collective victim rates, our understanding of the victimization of corporate entities should be enhanced. Another area mentioned is victim
targets, with reference to attractive targets and offender crimes in the aggregate, not to a specific victim-offender relationship. They believe that the
data generated by victimization surveys could lend themselves to analysis by
mathematical models, system analysis, or operation research.

There is also a possible emergence of a "victim public" as a result of
organized public concern with crime and victimization. This concern might
lead to public mobilization for protection against crime. Victimization
research may help "to examine methods for mobilizing the public to deal
with the crime problem as a community" (Wolfgang and Singer 1978, p.
387). Victimization surveys also can contribute to the understanding of
victim-offender relationships, by helping to find out who attacks whom or

who steals from whom. As mentioned earlier, victims often contribute to their own victimization. Wolfgang and Singer attempt to differentiate among the concepts of victim proneness, victim contribution to victimization, and victim provocation, and they emphasize the possible function of these factors in the criminal-justice process:

> The extent to which the victim's actions are responsible for his victimization might be considered in determining the extent of punishment for the offender and compensation to the victim. (Wolfgang and Singer 1978, p. 390)

Thus, this area may contribute to better criminal-justice administration and crime-prevention programs. Furthermore, this approach will increase our understanding of the biopsychosocial factors that play a part in determining an individual's chances of becoming a victim—a kind of research that can be conducted using aggregate data. Wolfgang and Singer also suggest examining the issue of victim recidivism. Victimization surveys can provide data in this area, and use of this information could contribute to victimological theory, to the computation of risk factors, and to prevention-policy decision making. This kind of analysis can shed light on the kinds of people who are victimized by various offenses. There is the additional possibility of using victimization data for research in victim compensation. Crime severity can be ascertained and correlated with amount of compensation. In terms of seriousness, compensation programs might also consider the characteristics of the victim in developing a fair system of restitution.

Victimological analysis can help in understanding the problems connected with the official treatment of victims by the authorities, as, for example, whether authorities contribute to the traumatic experiences of victims. Wolfgang and Singer (1978) mention some questions in this regard—such as whether or not personnel of the various criminal-justice agencies relate to victims in a sympathetic, professional, ahd helpful manner; whether victims are given proper information about procedures and about their rights; whether victims should receive compensation for time spent reporting to the police, giving testimony to the prosecutor, and being in the courtroom; and what the psychological effects of the victimization and the trial procedures are for the victims. Research into these questions can suggest legislative and judicial policy measures. As a reflection of the growing awareness of these problems, there are now several social programs that deal with victims, such as rape hot lines, victim counseling, victim advocacy, and victim-witness court programs.

Wolfgang and Singer (1978) also suggest that attention be paid to the indirect effects of victimization, which are neglected not only by the authorities but also by researchers. This topic might include the study of individuals who are seriously affected by the victimization of others, such as a husband whose wife was raped. This subject indicates the complexity of the victimization problem.

Another area of interest is connected with victims who are also offenders (for example, cheated gamblers in illegal gambling). As an extension of this area, research could be directed toward learning about individuals who become offenders as a result of their victimization, such as victims of frauds who learn how to defraud others. There are indications that the condition of being both an offender and a victim is very widespread, as shown by Wolfgang, Figlio, and Sellin (1972). They found that, in a birth cohort of males, 27 percent of those who were arrested during their juvenile years reported that they were also victims of violent crime, whereas only 11 percent of those who were not arrested had been victimized.

These considerations of the future development of victimization studies indicate only the beginnings of a fruitful and burgeoning area of study. In this book, we will employ victimization data in research on the macrosociological level, using aggregate demographic data. Research on this level of analysis has been widespread in criminology but has relied almost exclusively on official crime statistics. It started with studies of the geographic distribution of crime in various countries of Europe during the nineteenth century. Later, it was expanded to include a larger set of variables and led to the ecological study of the distribution of crime. The following chapter provides a brief review of some of these earlier studies of the ecological distribution of crime and victimization.

Urban Structural Analysis

Human Ecology and Crime

Human ecology is basically involved with the study of the relationships that exist among people who share a common habitat or territory and that are related to the character of that territory. The ecological approach to the study of crime is involved in the examination of the distribution of different types of crimes and crime rates among various spatial areas (Nettler 1978).

Nineteenth-Century Studies

The first studies analyzing the ecological patterns of crime were conducted in France and Belgium by Guerry and Quetelet during the nineteenth century. These studies were facilitated by the availability of systematic data on crime and criminals (Voss and Petersen 1971). Guerry (1833) analyzed the crime data of France for the period 1825-1830 by dividing the country into five regions, each with seventeen departments. The details of this analysis are described by Elmer (1933):

> He compiled data on various types of crime in each department and made interesting tables, maps, and comparisons based upon geographical location and considering age, sex, and instruction [education]. He classified crimes as crimes against the person and crimes against property. (pp. 64-65)

Guerry based his calculations on the number of people accused of crimes rather than on the number of people convicted by the courts. In Belgium, Quetelet (1842) also focused on geographic factors and their possible bearing on the distribution of crimes. He attempted to test empirically (on the basis of the geographical distribution of crime and other variables), questions that are still being asked, such as whether crime is due to poverty, lack of education, or population density.

Ecological studies of crime in the nineteenth century were also conducted in England. Rawson (1839), for example, analyzed the statistics available in England and Wales for the period 1835-1839 concerning the various kinds of offenses and their relationships to age and sex variables. Using the 1831 census he divided the counties into four groups, according to their major economic activities: agricultural, manufacturing, mining, and metropolitan. He concluded that the urban concentration of population, which creates crowded cities, is the major cause of crime. In reviewing these studies, Morris (1971) notes:

> Rawson qualifies for the title of social ecologist by virtue of his views that the regularity and pattern of social behavior is the result of the pattern of social institutions, which themselves vary between different districts. (p. 55)

Fletcher (1848) also used economic variables to distinguish various sections of England and Wales and to create what he termed "natural areas" for analysis (Levin and Lindesmith 1937). The main focus of his interest was to examine the relationship between education and crime. He studied what he called "indices to moral influences" and "indices to moral results." Indices to moral influences (independent variables) included dispersion of the population, real property in proportion to the population, persons of independent means in proportion to the population, and ignorance (writing). Indices to moral results (dependent variables) included crime, criminal commitments, improvident marriages, bastardy, pauperism, and deposits in banks in proportion to population. Fletcher concluded that densely populated areas have an effect of assembling rather than breeding an "excess of demoralization."

John Glyde (1856) conducted similar research during this period. His paper, "Localities of Crimes in Suffolk" (based on judicial data for 1848-1853), divided the county into smaller analytical units and examined the data accordingly. He focused on the hypothesis that crime increases with density of population, but he did not find a clear relationship. He further concluded that crime is not a result of the migration of people to towns. A few years later, Mayhew (1862) used official statistics in his work, *The Criminal Prisons of London*, to analyze the concentration of criminal offenses in different parts of London and certain counties of England and Wales.

Thus, the ecological approach to the study of crime has its origins in the works of nineteenth-century European researchers of crime rates and population statistics. This approach became much more prominent and sophisticated, however, in the twentieth century in the United States, beginning with sociologists connected with the University of Chicago (Faris 1967).

Twentieth-Century Studies

The first well-known systematic study of delinquency and ecological areas in a large city was started in 1921 by Shaw and McKay and was published in several books (1929, 1931, 1969). They analyzed the distribution of crime and delinquency in the natural areas of Chicago and related it to social-structural factors, such as physical status (population increase or decrease), economic status, and population composition (Voss and Petersen 1971). In their work, Shaw and McKay followed the ecological approach.[1] They found that high-crime-rate areas are characterized by high population mobility, economic dependency, physical deterioration, rented homes, and a heterogeneous population. Finestone (1976) summarized their findings as follows:

1. The rates of juvenile delinquents conformed to a regular spatial pattern. They were highest in the inner-city areas and tended to decline with distance from the center of the city.

2. The same spatial pattern was shown by many other indexes of social problems.

3. The spatial pattern of rates of delinquents showed considerable long-term stability even though the nationality makeup of the population in the inner-city areas changed greatly from decade to decade.

4. Within the inner-city areas the process of becoming delinquent occurred within a network of interpersonal relationships involving the family, the gang, and the neighborhood. (p. 25)

Since the 1950s, several large-scale human ecological studies have been conducted, focusing mainly on intracity analysis. Lander (1954), for example, studied the ecological correlates of juvenile delinquency in Baltimore, Bordua (1958-1959) replicated Lander's study in Detroit, and Chilton (1964) compared the Baltimore and Detroit studies with an ecological study of Indianapolis. Schmidt (1960a, 1960b) studied urban crime areas in Seattle.

In the president's *Task Force Report*, Wilks (1967) reviewed some of the major characteristics of the early ecological studies. She describes the major thrust of this approach:

The discovery of the spatial distributions of crime and delinquency rates and in some instances, the analysis of the relationship of these distributions to distributions of other attributes of population aggregates has been the aim of students of the ecology of crime and delinquency. (Wilks 1967, p. 138)

Wilks also distinguishes among the various types of ecological studies that deal with the differential distribution of crime rates. She suggests four different types of ecological studies: rural-urban differences, intracity differences, intercity differences, and regional differences.

Beasley and Antunes (1974) conducted an intracity study of Houston, using the number of offenses known to the police, to focus on the determinants of serious crime. They found (using a multivariate analysis) that the social-structural variables having the best predictive abilities were median income and population density.

Schuessler (1962) conducted a study, using Uniform Crime Reports (UCR) rates and census data, aimed at determining whether the variation in the crime rate of large American cities (100,000 population or more) could be statistically explained by a few social variables or whether a large number of factors would be required. Another task was to establish the sociological meanings of statistical factors that would emerge through the analysis. He concluded that the occurrence of crime is a function of social factors, that crimes should be grouped into several categories, and that individual differences cannot explain group differences.

In her intracity ecological study of crime in St. Louis, Boggs (1965) used indicators of social rank, urbanization, and racial segregation to analyze variations in the crime rates. On the basis of her research, she drew a distinction among the kinds of crime committed where the offender resides and those that attract offenders from other areas.

In his ecological study focusing on regional differences, Quinney (1966) analyzed the relationship between offense rates and population statistics. He found that crime rates vary with the structure of the population. Specifically, he concluded that structural variables affect crime rates differentially in rural, urban, and standard metropolitan statistical areas (SMSAs), that rural and urban areas seem to be more sensitive than SMSAs to these structural variables, and that offenses vary according to the degree that they correlate with structural variables and the degree that structural variables correlate with offenses.

In a recent intracity ecological study using police records, Block (1979) analyzed the patterns of homicide, robbery, and aggravated assault in the various neighborhoods of Chicago. He found that these three types of crimes are highest in neighborhoods where middle-class and very poor people live in close proximity. Social-class spatial proximity was the demographic variable that was most strongly related to crime rates.

During the 1950s and 1960s, several studies were published dealing with some of the methodological problems of the ecological approach (Jonassen 1949; Robinson 1950; Rosen and Turner 1967; Gordon 1967). Probably the most widely quoted is Robinson's article, "Ecological Correlations and the Behavior of Individuals." The importance of this article is its emphasis that ecological correlations are not equivalent to individual correlations. Although the article has become a widely cited classic, researchers often make conclusions regarding individuals on the basis of ecological correlations.

Some more recent studies focusing on intraurban analysis used reported information on residential burglary and residential robbery, as well as information collected from victims of crimes. Reppetto (1974) found that the major factors in the differential burglary rates among intracity areas are the location of the neighborhood, the level of affluence of the residents, and the vulnerability of the dwelling unit.

In his study of big-city crime rates, using Uniform Crime Report data, Skogan (1977a) focused on intercity variations in the distribution of crime. In a multi-city time-series analysis (covering 1946-1970), he found that Wirth's (1938) hypothesis that crime rates are highest in large, dense, and heterogeneous urban areas was supported using the 1970 data but was not supported for the earlier years. Thus, the concentration of crime in these areas seems to be a relatively recent development, very likely an outcome of post-World War II suburbanization, when large numbers of the white middle class left the central cities.

In the 1970s and early 1980s, several ecological studies of crime and delinquency were conducted by geographers (Harries 1971, 1973, 1974, 1976, 1980; Harries and Brunn 1978; Herbert 1977; Georges and Harries, forthcoming; and others). The ecological studies of crime and delinquency by geographers are based on interests similar to those of other social scientists. Harries and Brunn (1978), for example, explain the importance of place in the criminal-justice process:

> When spatial variations in laws, law enforcement efficiency, prosecutor toughness, jail and prison conditions, disposition time for cases, judicial competence, jury role and selection processes, and the effectiveness of probation and parole systems are considered, one can begin to develop an appreciation for the role of what may be loosely called place in the judicial process. (pp. 3-4)

With the development of the National Crime Surveys (NCS) during the second half of the 1960s and the 1970s, a new source of data became available for ecological studies of crime. As mentioned earlier, one reason for using these data is that they seem to present more complete and more accurate information on the amount of crime, the types of offenses, and other details of the criminal act—such as the race, sex, and age of victims. Pope (1979), for example, conducted an intracity study comparing neighborhoods and their household-victimization rates. He found that this kind of victimization varies with population characteristics—mainly the age structure of the neighborhood. On the intercity level, among others, Boland (1976) studied robbery victimization in twenty-six large American cities; Hindelang (1976) analyzed victimization in eight large cities; and Shichor, Decker, and O'Brien (1979) analyzed urban population density (population per square mile) and victimization patterns in twenty-six large cities.

Hindelang's (1976) detailed analysis produced several interesting findings regarding the characteristics of the victims of various crimes, the characteristics of the victimization situation, the victim-offender relationship, the consequences of the different types of victimization, and some differences in the victimization patterns of various crimes. Although his study used aggregate data, he did not use urban structural variables in his analysis, which limits the usefulness of the study for our purposes.

Some Methodological Issues

Use of Aggregate-Level Data

As indicated by the preceding brief review, there is a long-standing tradition of research concerning intercity variations in crime rates. This tradition is not diminished by the fact that it is based on aggregate-level data. What is important to remember in considering the literature reviewed throughout this book is that the relationship between citywide structural characteristics and citywide victimization rates may not be the same as those found at other levels of analysis, such as block level or census-tract level (see Alker 1969; Slatin 1969; Roncek 1975). The analysis of these data, however, allows us to investigate the relationships between these characteristics and rates of criminal victimization at one important level of social aggregation—the level of central cities. This is the level of much theorizing in criminalogy (for example, Wirth 1938; Shaw and McKay 1969; Skogan 1977a).

Urban Structural Variables

The urban structural variables investigated in this study are population density (population per square mile), crowding (the percentage of households with 1.01 or more residents per room), median income, median education, percentage of the population who are white, percentage unemployed, percentage foreign-born, percentage on public assistance, percentage elderly (65 years and over), and percentage between the ages of 12 and 24. These structural characteristics were selected according to the following criteria: (1) indications from previous studies or theories that they are related to crime rates, (2) relatively low intercorrelations with other structural characteristics, and (3) availability. To meet the first of these criteria, we relied on our own judgment and a survey of the criminological literature (for example, Clinard 1968; Sutherland and Cressey 1978; Booth, Johnson, and Choldin 1977). The second criterion was employed to keep the structural characteristics reasonably independent of one another. If we used the percentage of the population in blue-collar jobs, the percentage in white-collar jobs, and the percentage in professional jobs as three separate structural characteristics, for example, not only would they correlate strongly but they would be somewhat redundant measures of the occupational structure of the city. Finally, the availability of this information in government publications partially dictated our choice of which structural characteristics to examine.

The structural characteristics examined include two measures of ethnic diversity (percentage white and percentage foreign-born), four measures of economic well-being (median income, median education, percentage on public assistance, and percentage unemployed), two measures of population density (population per square mile and percentage of household with 1.01 or more residents per room), and two measures of age distribution (percentage 65 years and over and percentage aged 12 to 24).

Sampled Cities: A Limitation

National Crime Surveys have been conducted in only twenty-six cities (A second survey has been taken in thirteen of them to provide a measure of change over time.) For eight of the cities we examined, victimizations are reported for the period between April 1, 1974, and May 31, 1975 (Atlanta, Baltimore, Cleveland, Dallas, Denver, Newark, Portland, and St. Louis); for five of the cities the period corresponds roughly to calendar year 1974 (Chicago, Detroit, Los Angeles, New York, and Philadelphia); and for thirteen of the cities the period corresponds roughly to the calendar year 1973 (Boston, Buffalo, Cincinnati, Houston, Miami, Milwaukee, Minneapolis, New Orleans, Oakland, Pittsburgh, San Diego, San Francisco, and Washington, D.C.). Although it is probably safe to assume that no major shifts in the structural characteristics of these cities occurred between 1973 and 1974—and thus we may compare these characteristics across data collected for these years—the major limiting factor for our structural analysis is the small size of the sample, only twenty-six cases. This severely limits the number of structural characteristics that may be used to predict victimization rates in any analysis. It is a mathematical necessity, for example, that, with twenty-five such variables, the researcher can predict perfectly the victimization rates for twenty-six cities. Furthermore, using ten such variables from a population in which all correlations between these variables and victimization rates were zero, they would be expected to produce a multiple correlation of .63 (R^2 = .40). Thus, there are problems with using multivariate analyses with only twenty-six cases. In order to cope with this problem, our approach has been to look for clear and recurrent patterns in the relationships among structural characteristics, as well as to perform analyses with few independent variables. The price of using the latter strategy is the sacrifice of the simultaneous statistical control over several structural characteristics in some of the anlayses reported. As will be seen in the following chapters, however, many compelling and suggestive patterns have been found in the analysis of the NCS data. Some of these patterns bring into question several long-standing empirical generalizations concerning the relationships between certain structural characteristics of cities and rates of criminal victimization; at the same time, some new ones are suggested.

Note

1. According to Hawley (1981), "human ecology seeks its explanations among variables that are structural properties, demographic attributes, and features of environment, including interactions with other systems (p. 10).

Victimization Surveys: A Comparison of Reported Crime Rates and Victimization Rates

Uniform Crime Reports and National Crime Surveys

Although many procedures may be used for collecting data regarding the extent of criminal behavior, only two methods have been used to obtain data from a large number of U.S. cities: consulting official statistics based on the reports of law-enforcement agencies and surveying the victims of crimes. Use of the official statistics is by far the older of the two procedures. The first systematic attempt to collect data for U.S. cities according to this procedure was initiated by the International Association of Chiefs of Police (IACP) in the late 1920s. Their procedures were formalized in 1930 under the supervision of the Federal Bureau of Investigation, thus establishing the Uniform Crime Reports (UCR).[1]

From 1930 until the late 1960s, these reports were the only systematic source of crime-rate data for U.S. cities. Doubts concerning the validity of these official rates have been expressed by several authors, however. The major criticisms have focused on three areas: (1) the victim's role in reporting crimes to the police, (2) organizational factors that impede accurate reporting, and (3) the role of the individual officer in reporting crime.

There are many reasons that victims do not report crimes to the police:

1. A victim might not realize that an offense has been committed.
2. There may be no victim in the usual sense of the word (victimless crimes).
3. A victim might fear reprisal.
4. A victim might fear self-incrimination or incrimination of close relatives or friends.
5. A victim might fear the personal consequences of the criminal-justice proceedings, such as cross-examination, public condemnation, and publicity.
6. A victim might not want to lose working time.
7. The offense might not seem severe.
8. A victim might not believe that the offender will be apprehended and punished.
9. A victim might be unable to identify the offender.
10. A victim might be uninsured or unaware of victim-compensation programs and thus would lack a monetary incentive to report crimes.

Many of these factors are discussed in more detail by Levine (1976) and Walker (1971).

Organizational factors that impede the accurate reporting of crime include the following:

1. Available police resources do not make it economically feasible to handle a large volume of minor offenses.
2. According to Walker (1971), "too many prosecutions for trivial offenses might alienate citizens on whom police can normally rely for help" (p. 17).
3. The large number of autonomous law-enforcement agencies leads to a great variety of law-enforcement policies and practices (Goldstein 1960; Greenwood and Wadycki 1973).
4. Political and budgetary considerations affect a police department's reporting of crime (Seidman and Couzens 1974; Milakovich and Weis 1975; Maltz 1977).

Factors that impede accurate reporting of crime on the part of the individual police officer include the following:

1. Personal preferences and biases (Black 1970; Seidman and Couzens 1974);
2. Situational factors, such as deference of the offender toward the police officer and demands by the victim for formal actions (Piliavin and Briar 1964; Wilson 1968);
3. Pressure for productivity, as measured by activity (Rubenstein 1973).

Generally, it is argued that a substantial number of crimes are not reported in the UCR but nevertheless contribute to "the dark figure of crime" (Biderman and Reiss 1967).

The cogency of these criticisms increased interest in the role of the victim (Wolfgang and Ferracuti 1962; Pokorny 1965; Fooner 1967). The establishment of victim-compensation programs and the advances in survey-research methods contributed to a growing interest in the idea of victimization surveys. It was thought that these surveys would "provide more reliable information about the frequency of crime" (Skogan 1976, p. xvii). Improved validity was expected to result from these surveys because (1) they provide a standard description of crime, which cuts across jurisdictional boundaries, thus providing comparable data from different geographical areas; (2) they offer a more complete coverage of crime, especially crimes considered too minor to report; (3) the accuracy of the reported event should be greater, since the victim is closer to the criminal act than anyone else except the criminal; and (4) the reporting of crime is made easier, in that there is no loss of working time and the victim does not have to initiate contact with the police.

The first of the major victimization surveys was conducted for the President's Commission on Law Enforcement and Administration of Justice. A pilot study was conducted in Washington, D.C.,[2] and a national survey was later administered by the National Opinion Research Center.[3] Results from these studies indicated that crimes were reported about twice as often in surveys as one would have expected from UCR figures. This finding, coupled with the fact that, during the early 1970s, the Law Enforcement Assistance Administration (LEAA) was funding its Impact Cities Program and needed a valid procedure by which to evaluate the success of its programs, led to the collection of victimization data by the U.S. Census Bureau on victimization in eight impact cities.[4] These cities were first surveyed in 1973 and then again in 1974. This marked the beginning of the National Crime Surveys (NCS). In 1975, similar surveys were conducted in another eighteen cities. Thus, comparable victimization surveys have been conducted in twenty-six large U.S. central cities.[5]

The victimization surveys that were initiated with such high hopes for success have come under some severe criticisms (Hood and Sparks 1970; Penick and Owens 1976; Levine 1976; Wolgang and Singer 1978). Several questions have been raised regarding their accuracy as a measure of criminal behavior.

One of these questions concerns the seriousness (or lack of seriousness) of the crimes reported on victimization surveys. Skogan (1977b) argues that the surveys elicit information on a large volume of petty crimes and that they do not add significantly to knowledge of serious crimes: "The pool of unreported crime consists mainly of minor property offenses. Unreported crimes against persons appear to be of less social significance than those which are brought to the attention of the police" (p. 49).

Another problem area concerns respondent accuracy. Penick and Owens (1976) discuss the results of several studies dealing with the telescoping of the reports of criminal events.[6] The net effect of telescoping is to increase the amount of reported victimizations. They also discuss the results of reverse record checks. This technique investigates recall among respondents who reported to the police that they were victimized. These studies indicate, for example, that between one-third and two-thirds of the assaults reported to the police are not reported to the interviewers.

It has also been noted that there is false reporting by respondents because of mistaken interpretation of incidents as crimes, intentional false reporting, and omission of reporting (for example, reluctance to report victimizations committed by relatives or close friends). Finally, certain segments of the population are systematically excluded from the survey, such as commuters and tourists who move out of the area before the survey is conducted (Nelson 1978). In addition, a potential problem with all surveys is the existence of interviewer biases and coder mistakes (Levine 1976).

All these weaknesses in both the UCR and NCS city data would lead one to expect that the crime rates based on officially reported crimes or surveyed crime would differ. An additional reason for expecting the two sets of rates to differ is that they are based on slightly different populations. The NCS records crimes that occurred to residents of the city who are 12 years of age or older. These crimes may or may not have occurred within the city. The UCR records crimes that occurred within the city limits, regardless of the respondent's age or residence. Thus, crimes that happen to residents, workers, tourists, shoppers, and so forth, are all included in the UCR rates.

Absolute Differences in UCR and NCS Estimated Crime Rates

A major finding of the NCS was a relatively high crime rate in comparison to the crime rate based on UCR data. This difference has been examined by a number of authors (Skogan 1974, 1976; Booth, Johnson, and Choldin 1977; Decker 1977). Decker, for example, compared the mean rates for all twenty-six cities involved in the NCS on rape, robbery, aggravated assault, personal larceny, burglary, and motor-vehicle theft. He found that the mean crime rates differ significantly ($p < 0005$), depending on whether they are estimated using NCS or UCR data. The only exception is the mean rate for motor-vehicle theft ($p > 05$). The differences in the estimated crime rates for these cities are very large, as can be seen in table 3-1. Furthermore, as

Table 3-1
Differences in the Mean Rates Based on UCR and NCS Estimates for Twenty-six Cities

| | Mean Rate (per 100,000) | | t | Ratio of NCS/UCR |
	NCS	UCR	Value	Mean Rates
Rape	137	50	8.05*	2.74
Robbery	1621	582	9.98*	2.79
Aggravated assault	766	360	5.28*	2.13
Larceny	9581	2737	8.92*	3.50
Burglary	6187	2065	13.64*	3.00
Motor-vehicle theft	1073	1186	−1.68**	.90

Source: Adapted from Decker (1977, p. 51).
*$p < .0005$.
**$p > .05$.

the last column of the table indicates, the rates based on NCS data are all more than twice as large as those based on the UCR data; the only exception is the rate for motor-vehicle theft. (We will argue later that people are motivated to report this crime to police for insurance purposes.)

Although it is well established that the UCR and NCS data provide very different estimates of the absolute level of criminal activity, it has been hoped that they both might still prove to be useful indicators of the same underlying dimension—criminal activity. Ennis (1967), for example, noted that the rank order of rates of index crimes for the National Opinion Research Center (NORC) victimization-survey estimates of crime rates and the UCR figures were similar, leading him to conclude that "this lends substantial credence that the survey and the UCR are describing the same universe of events" (pp. 8-9). Thus, although the estimated crime rates might differ, depending on which estimate was employed, they could still provide a relevant yardstick on which to measure the *relative amount* of crime in different cities. For this purpose, the two indexes need not equal each other in any specific case to be perfectly valid as indicators of the relative amount of crime in various cities. Furthermore, if the two indexes were proportional (for example, the NCS index for rape is always 2.74 times the UCR rate across cities), the same substantive conclusions would be reached when using analytic techniques based on variances and covariances, such as correlation and regression analyses.

Thus, in the analysis that follows, we are concerned not with whether NCS and UCR crime rates agree in terms of the absolute amount of crime (they clearly do not, as table 3-1 indicates), but rather with whether they agree in terms of the relative amounts of crime. This is a question that is best investigated using the classic notions of validity assessment.

An Empirical Assessment of the Validity of NCS and UCR Rates

Assessing the validity of a measure is, at best, a difficult task that provides only tentative answers. Only in rare situations—where a criterion measure exists—can the results of a validation study be more than suggestive. Two major classes of procedures are used to evaluate the validity of variables. The first of these is based on an evaluation of the content of the measure—that is, an examination to determine if it adequately reflects the content of the variable one wants to measure. In attempting to ascertain whether or not an individual was the victim of an assault, for example, the NCS interviewers asked: "Did anyone beat you up, attack you or hit you with something such as a rock or bottle?" "Were you knifed, shot at, or attacked with some other weapon by anyone at all?" "Did anyone threaten to beat you up or threaten you with a knife, gun, or some other weapon, not including telephone threats?'' and so on (U.S. Department of Justice, 1976a, p. 141). The questions were constructed to cover the concept of victimization by assault. Whether or not this attempt was successful is a question about content validity.

The second class of procedures involves statistical assessments of validity. These procedures usually rely on the computation of correlation coefficients between two (or more) variables. In the simplest case, criterion validity, the validity of a measure is ascertained by correlating it with a direct (true) measure of the concept under investigation—for example, the correlation of reported income-tax payments with actual tax payments (Zellitz, Wrightsman, and Cook 1976). Unfortunately, such comparisons are seldom possible, because adequate criterion measures do not exist; that is, no measure of the "true" crime rate exists. Other empirical comparisons can be made, however, to support the validity of a measure. In this chapter we are concerned with two of these procedures: convergent validation (Campbell and Fiske 1959) and nomological validation (Selltiz, Wrightsman, and Cook 1976). Convergent validation is based on the argument that two variables that validly measure the same concept should correlate highly; that is, if the rate of burglary reported by NCS and UCR are measuring the same phenomenon (true burglary rates), there should be a strong positive correlation between these reported rates across central cities. Nomological validation is based on the argument that two variables (not measuring the same concept) that theory suggests are related should correlate highly if they are both valid measures; that is, if median income of cities is held to be correlated with crime rates, there should be a correlation between the median income of cities and the UCR and NCS rates across cities.

Both these validation procedures can provide support for the validity of a particular measure, but they do not provide conclusive evidence. If two variables designed to measure the same concept are not highly correlated, it may be a result of a number of factors; for example, the first measure might be invalid, the second measure might be invalid, or both measures might be invalid. A strong positive correlation between these same two variables, however, may mean that both are valid or that both are related to some third variable that is unrelated to the concept under consideration—a spurious correlation (Althauser and Heberlein 1970; Althauser 1974). It is conceivable, for example, that victims in certain cities are more likely to report crimes both to the police and to NCS interviewers.

The problems associated with nomological validation are even more complicated. If two measures predicted by theory to be related are not, it may be that the first measure is invalid, the second measure is invalid, both measures are invalid, or the theory is incorrect. A high correlation between these two variables, however, may mean that both are valid or that both are related to a third variable that is not related to the concept under consideration.

Bearing these cautions in mind, we would still argue that, when a measure has a high degree of convergent or nomological validity, it is a positive factor in the evaluation of its validity. Furthermore, if there is a low degree of convergent or nomological validity, it raises questions about the validity of the measure. We will assess here the convergent and nomological validity of both the UCR and NCS rates.

Procedures

The analysis focuses on two sets of relationships: (1) the correlation between NCS victimization rates and UCR crime rates and (2) a comparison of the relative strength of the correlations of NCS victimization rates and UCR crime rates with several theoretically relevant independent variables. NCS and UCR rates for six crimes (robbery, burglary, rape, aggravated assault, personal larceny, and motor-vehicle theft) are available for twenty-six large American central cities. These cities serve as our unit of analysis. Victimization rates are based on NCS data, compiled by the U.S. Bureau of the Census for the Law Enforcement Assistance Administration (U.S. Department of Justice 1975, 1976a, 1976b). Reported crimes are based on UCR data, published by the Federal Bureau of Investigation (Federal Bureau of Investigation 1974, 1975). We included in our study all victimization rates and crime rates for which comparable index crimes are reported in both the UCR and NCS. UCR data for 1973 were used for thirteen cities for which the NCS recorded victimizations occurring during 1973. Similarly, UCR data for 1974 were used for thirteen other cities in which victimization surveys took place from approximately April 1974 to April 1975. Since the UCR rates for both burglary and robbery combine commercial and personal incidents of these crimes, it was necessary to compute the NCS rates (per thousand population) for these crimes by appropriately combining household and commercial burglaries and personal and commercial robberies from the NCS publications. Data on the independent variables (structural characteristics of central cities) for the twenty-six cities were obtained from the U.S. Bureau of the Census (1973). The structural characteristics were selected according to the following criteria (mentioned in chapter 2): (1) indications from previous studies or theories that they are related to crime rates, (2) relatively low intercorrelations with other structural characteristics, and (3) availability.

The third criterion needs little comment, since it obviously would be impractical to use measures that are not available for these central cities. As mentioned in chapter 2, to meet the first criterion, we relied on our own

judgment and a survey of the criminological literature. We have not attempted to predict the direction of the relationship between each of the independent variables and the crime rate, because there are disagreements
among criminologists and among research studies concerning the direction
of the effects of several structural correlates of crime. Is density positively
related to crime rates, for example, as Wirth (1938), Shaw and McKay
(1969), and Beasley and Antunes (1974) suggest, or is it negatively related
to crime rates, as suggested by Kvalseth (1977) and Boland (1976). It could
also be positively related to some types of crimes and negatively related to
others (Shichor, Decker, and O'Brien 1979). Is the general affluence of an
area negatively associated with crime rates, as suggested by those who
argue that poverty is a breeding ground for criminals (for example, Cohen
1955; Miller 1958), or is it positively associated, as suggested by those who
argue that criminals focus on more affluent targets (for example, Reppetto
1974; Boggs 1965). Although researchers have been unable to evaluate
conclusively the relative merits of all these arguments (for a recent review,
see Tittle et al. 1978), there is general agreement that urban crime rates
should correlate with important urban structural characteristics.
Therefore, in the assessment of the nomological validity of UCR and NCS
crime rates, we have decided to employ variables such as population density and median education, which are generally believed to affect crime
rates, but not attempt to predict the direction of the relationship.

The second criterion was employed to keep the tests of nomological
validity reasonably independent. If, for example, we employed the percentage of the population in blue-collar jobs, the percentage in white-
collar jobs, and the percentage in professional jobs as three separate, independent variables, and if one of these correlated more strongly with
NCS rates than with UCR rates, the tests involving the other two independent variables would likely show the same pattern of results. The independent variables in this study are density (population per square mile),
crowding (percentage of households with 1.01 or more residents per
room), percentage white, median income, percentage unemployed, percentage foreign-born, percentage on public assistance, and percentage between the ages of 12 and 24.

Table 3-2 presents a correlation matrix for the independent variables,
which shows that only four correlations are .50 or greater (in absolute
value) among the independent variables, and that it would be possible to
eliminate these by dropping the variables "percentage aged 12 to 24" and
"median income" from the analysis. We have decided to keep these
variables in the analysis, because there are strong grounds—both
theoretical and from previous research—to suggest that they are associated
with crime rates.

Table 3-2
Correlations between the Structural Characteristics of Twenty-six Central Cities

	Density	Crowding	Percentage White	Median Income	Percentage Unemployed	Percentage Foreign-born	Percentage on Public Assistance	Percentage Aged 12-24
Density	1.00	.10	-.20	-.04	.00	.40	.38	-.50
Crowding		1.00	-.48	-.67	-.27	.48	.43	-.39
Percentage white			1.00	.37	.05	.16	-.32	.14
Median income				1.00	.12	-.17	-.60	.20
Percentage unemployed					1.00	.12	.32	-.12
Percentage foreign-born						1.00	.40	-.65
Percentage on public assistance							1.00	-.27
Percentage aged 12-24								1.00

Findings

In this section, we first examine the convergent validity of the UCR and NCS crime rates and then examine their nomological validity relative to each other. Table 3-3 presents the results of the tests for convergent validity. The convergent validity of the measures varies, depending on the type of crime involved. There is good agreement, for example, between the NCS and UCR rates for motor-vehicle theft ($r = .90$); in fact, these two measures share 81 percent of their variance in common. The UCR and NCS rates for robbery and burglary are also highly correlated, although these measures share only 62 percent and 48 percent of their variance in common. The convergent validity of the rates for the remaining three types of crime are very low, however, ranging from .32 to -.39. We can conclude from this table that the convergent validity for at least three of the six measures is very low. This raises questions about the validity of both the UCR and NCS measures for at least these three types of crime.

Table 3-4 presents the results of our tests of nomological validity for both the NCS and UCR crime rates. In comparing the two sets of crime-rate measures, we report the number of zero-order correlations between the independent variables and the crime rates that reach the .01, .05, and .10 levels of statistical significance. Although the .10 level of statistical significance is less often reported than either the .01 or .05 levels, it seems appropriate in the present study (if interpreted with caution), given the strong possibility of type 2 errors (that is, failure to detect a real population difference) when the sample size is small. For the NCS rates, nine of forty-eight correlations are significant at the .01 level, sixteen of forty-eight are significant at the .05 level or better, and twenty-three of forty-eight are significant at the .10 level or better. For the UCR rates, six of forty-eight correlations are significant at the .01 level, eleven of forty-eight are significant at the .05 level or better, and twelve of forty-eight are significant at the .10 level or better. As a set, then, the nomological validity of NCS rates ap-

Table 3-3
Correlation between Victimization and UCR Rates for Various Types of Crimes in Twenty-six Cities

Type of Crime	r_{xy}	r_{xy}^2	Significance Level
Motor-vehicle theft	.90	.81	.001
Robbery	.79	.62	.001
Burglary	.69	.48	.001
Personal larceny	.32	.10	.054
Rape	.01	.00	NS
Aggravated assault	- .39	—	NS

Table 3-4
Correlation of UCR and NCS Rates with Important Structural Characteristics of Twenty-six Cities

	Motor-Vehicle Theft		Robbery		Burglary		Personal Larceny		Rape		Aggravated Assault	
	UCR	NCS	UCR	NCS	UCR	NCS	UCR	NCS	UCR	NCS	UCR	NCS
Density	NS	NS	.51*	.55*	NS	-.54*	.48	-.54**	NS	-.48**	NS	-.44**
Crowding	NS	NS	NS	NS	NS	-.33***	NS	-.64*	NS	.49**	.58*	-.65*
Percentage white	NS	NS	-.70*	-.37***	NS	NS	NS	.56*	-.52*	.34***	-.50*	.43**
Median income	NS	NS	NS	NS	NS	NS	NS	.61*	NS	NS	-.48**	.43**
Percentage unemployed	NS	NS	NS	NS	NS	NS	NS	NS	NS	NS	NS	NS
Percentage foreign-born	NS	NS	NS	NS	NS	NS	NS	-.37***	NS	NS	.37***	-.45**
Percentage on public assistance	.53*	NS	.49**	.34***	NS	NS	NS	-.51*	NS	NS	.48**	-.41**
Percentage aged 12-24	NS	NS	NS	NS	NS	NS	NS	.52*	NS	.34***	-.47**	.34***

NS = not significant.

*p < .01
**p < .05
***p < .10

pears to be somewhat superior to that of the UCR rates, although, for most crimes (motor-vehicle theft, robbery, burglary, and aggravated assault), the NCS and UCR rates have a similar degree of nomological validity.

Discussion

The pattern of convergent validity noted in table 3-3 is consistent with validity checks done by using two other research designs. The first design involves asking NCS respondents whether or not they have reported to the police the crimes that they reported to the interviewer. The second research design is a reverse-record check. According to this design, a sample is selected of people who reported crimes to the police. These people are then interviewed in a survey, and their responses to questions concerning victimization are then compared to what is known from police records.

Results from these designs are consistent with those of our tests for convergent validity. When those who reported being victimized on the 1976 National Crime Surveys (U.S. Department of Justice 1977) were asked if they had reported these crimes to the police, for example, the percentage of victimizations reported to the police ranged from a low of 26 percent for personal larceny without contact to a high of 87 percent for commercial robbery. Burglaries (household and commercial combined), robberies (household and commercial combined), and motor-vehicle theft were reported to the police more than 50 percent of the time. These three crimes show the greatest convergent validity in table 3-3. Personal larceny and aggravated assault, however, were reported less than 50 percent of the time to the police. Even though 53 percent of the respondents who state that they were victimized by rape say they reported this crime to the police, the convergent validity of this crime is very low. Aside from the problems regarding reporting rape to police or interviewers, the low level of convergent validity for rape may result from the fact that the incidence of rape, as reported in NCS, is based on so few cases as to make that rate highly unreliable.

In reviewing studies using reverse-record-check designs, Penick and Owens (1976) state: "In general reporting of burglary and robbery was greater than reporting of theft, and all three of these types of property crime were more likely to be mentioned to interviewers than were assaults" (p. 39). The studies they reviewed did not include motor-vehicle theft. Thus, the results of the reverse-record checks parallel our findings, in which property-crime rates for UCR and NCS measures show a higher level of agreement than do those for aggravated assault.

The results in table 3-4 are arranged so that crimes showing higher levels of convergent validity are on the left and those showing less convergent validity are on the right. Motor-vehicle theft—the crime showing the greatest convergent validity—surprisingly has rather weak correlations with the eight urban structural characteristics we examined. Only one of the sixteen correlations is significant at the .10 level. If one is convinced of the accuracy of reporting motor-vehicle theft to both police and interviewers (and there is reason to be convinced), these results may indicate that the rate of motor-vehicle theft is not highly related to these urban structural characteristics. Robbery, which has the next highest convergent validity, shows a similar pattern of relationships for both the NCS and UCR rates and urban characteristics. Six of the sixteen correlations are significant at the .10 level or better, and many of these are rather large. More important, the direction of the relationships (positive or negative) is the same for both the NCS and the UCR data. This adds to our confidence that NCS and UCR rates for robbery are valid.

The next crime, burglary, has only two significant correlations with the eight urban characteristics—the correlations between the NCS measure of the burglary rate and population density and crowding.

The next two crimes, personal larceny and rape, favor the NCS over the UCR measure. Only two of the sixteen correlations between UCR rates and urban characteristics are significant at the .10 level or better. For the NCS measure, however, eleven of the sixteen correlations are significant at the .10 level. For these two crimes, which show a very low level of convergent validity, the tests for nomological validity favor the NCS measure. Finally, the rates for aggravated assault, which show the least convergent validity, have a most perplexing pattern. Both the NCS and UCR measures show a high degree of nomological validity. Six of the UCR rates and seven of the NCS rates are correlated significantly at the .10 level or better with the eight urban characteristics. In each of the six cases in which both NCS and UCR rates are significantly correlated for the same characteristic, however, the correlations are in the opposite direction. This makes it difficult to assess the relative validity of these two measures of aggravated assault. As indicated earlier, this crime shows the least consistency in reverse-record checks and is least often reported to police by those interviewed in the NCS surveys.

Summary

We began this chapter with a review of many of the problems with crime-rate data provided by the UCR. These problems with official crime statistics make the idea of victimization surveys very appealing. We then discussed some of the limitations of victimization surveys. It has been clear for some time now that the UCR crime rates are much lower than those reported in victimization surveys. This means that conclusions concerning the absolute amount of crime will vary greatly depending on which of these two indexes is used. The two indexes might still reflect the relative amount of crime accurately, however, and thus would be useful in correlation and regression analyses. This point of view finds support in an article by Skogan (1974), based on an analyses of UCR and NCS data for ten cities. Our own investigation of this question—based on an assessment of the convergent and nomological validity of these two measures—yields less sanguine results. Regarding the degree to which the two measures of crime correlate across cities, for example, it was found that, for the six types of crimes examined, only three showed even a moderate degree of convergent validity—motor-vehicle theft, robbery, and burglary. The low correlations between NCS and UCR rates for the three other crimes—personal larceny, rape, and aggravated assault—raises questions about the validity of both the UCR- and NCS-based rates. In an attempt to resolve questions concerning the relative validity of these two measures, their nomological validity was examined by correlating each measure with a number of urban structural characteristics that are thought to be correlated with the true rate of crime. This analysis shows that, overall, the NCS rates exhibit a greater degree of nomological validity than do the UCR rates; however, this finding is based mainly on the results for the crimes of personal larceny and rape. The UCR had a greater number of statistically significant correlations ($p < .10$) than the NCS rates for only one of the six types of crimes.

This analysis raises some questions for which there are no easy answers. It would be interesting, for example, to speculate about the reasons for the rather strong negative correlation between NCS and UCR rates for aggravated assault ($-.39$), as reported in table 3-3. Although it is easy to suggest reasons that the UCR and NCS rates might differ in absolute terms for the cities in our analysis, we have yet to discover a convincing explanation of the observed tendency for cities with a higher-than-average official rate (UCR) for aggravated assault to have lower-than-average victimization rates (NCS). The same comment applies to the correlations in table 3-4, which are in opposite directions, depending on which crime-rate measure is used; for example, the "percentage white" is negatively related to the UCR measure of aggravated assault and positively related to the NCS measure. These and other inconsistent relationships suggest that further investigations into the meaning of both official and survey-based rates are needed.

These findings—as well as those of Booth, Johnson, and Choldin (1977), Decker (1977), and Nelson (1978)—should be sobering for those who use either NCS or UCR data in their research. Although researchers may have little choice in the selection of available data sources that are relevant to their research goals, we believe that, when such a choice is available, the NCS rates are probably more valid than the UCR rates. This conclusion is based on the results reported here, and on our assessment of possible biasing factors in each of the two measures. There is room for disagreement on this point, however. The validity of the UCR and NCS measures is an especially important issue to criminological researchers, since most of the research involving cities, SMSAs, and states as the units of analysis rely on one or the other of these two measures. The findings of these studies can be no more valid than the data on which they are based.

In the next chapter, we will use the NCS data to develop a three-category classification of criminal victimization. This classification is found to have a high degree of empirical consistency (when tested using eight urban structural characteristics) and seems to have a greater explanatory power than the most commonly employed categorization of crimes.

Notes

1. See Maltz (1977) for a fascinating historical account of the development of the Uniform Crime Reports.

2. See Biderman and Reiss's (1967) report on their pilot study in the District of Columbia.

3. See P. H. Ennis's (1967) report on the first in-depth, nationwide survey of criminal victimization in the United States.

4. The eight cities were Atlanta, Baltimore, Cleveland, Dallas, Denver, Newark, Portland, and St. Louis.

5. The list of twenty-six cities appears in appendix C. These surveys are not to be confused with the National Crime Panel Surveys (NCPS), which are also conducted for the LEAA by the Census Bureau, but are designed to be administered to a representative sample of United States citizens who are 12 years of age and over.

6. Telescoping "refers to the phenomenon whereby a respondent acknowledges an actual event to the interviewer but reports the date of its occurrence inaccurately" (Penick and Owens 1976, p. 42).

4

An Empirical Classification of Criminal Victimization

Social scientists use the process of typification and classification to organize and order information and data for building knowledge within an academic discipline. McKinney refers to the conscious use of this process by social scientists as the constructed type of classification. The primary function of a constructed classification is to develop a set of types that "identify, simplify, and order the concrete data so that they may be described in terms that make them comparable" (McKinney 1966, p. 216). In addition, a classification should contribute to a body of knowledge by linking empirical data to a theoretical framework and should enhance the understanding of a subject by suggesting new lines of inquiry, suggesting new relationships, deriving new hypotheses, and revising theories. A number of social scientists have discussed the nature of classifications and have distinguished between the conceptual basis and methodological issues for classification construction (Wood 1969; Winch 1947; McKinney 1966; Barton 1955; Lazarsfeld 1972; Hage 1972; Schrag 1967).

Criminologists have also employed classifications in their attempt to make sense of criminological data. Existing classifications in the field can be grouped into several categories, including those that concern types of offenders (for example, Roebuck 1967); types of inmates (for example, Schrag 1961; Sykes 1958; Garabedian 1964); motives for criminal offenses (for example, Bonger 1961); types of offenses (for example, Balkin 1979); types of victims (for example, Von Hentig 1948; Mendelsohn 1956; Wolfgang and Singer 1978); and some more complex classifications that use several factors, such as criminal behavior, role careers, and intent (Clinard and Quinney 1973; Gibbons 1975; Glaser 1972).

In this chapter, we present a classification of crimes (criminal violations) that distinguishes among different types of crime and is derived from NCS data (U.S. Department of Justice, 1975, 1976*a*, 1976*b*). These categories, or types, were derived in a way similar to the grounded-theory approach advocated by Glaser and Strauss (1967). The basic feature of this approach is "the discovery of theory from data systematically obtained from social research" (p. 2). Glaser and Strauss suggest that the theoretical relevance of concepts be demonstrated by whether they yield consistent and meaningful patterns of results. Here we employ the same NCS data and the same set of structural characteristics used in the previous chapter to generate an empirically grounded classification of crimes. (See appendix A for a description of the NCS research design and appendix B for the definitions of the ten different crimes.)

Discovering a Classification for Crimes

Our initial classification resulted from an attempt to explain the pattern of relationships between population density and victimization rates for the ten types of crimes represented in the NCS (see chapter 5). The classification of these ten crimes according to their empirical and theoretical relationship to population density yielded three categories of crime:

1. Property crimes with contact—robbery with injury, robbery without injury, and personal larceny with contact—were all positively correlated with population density. These are all property crimes that bring the offender and the victim into direct contact.
2. Property crimes without contact—household burglary, household larceny, and personal larceny without contact—were negatively correlated with population density. These are all property crimes in which the offender and the victim typically are not in direct contact. Another property crime without contact—motor-vehicle theft—was not significantly correlated with population density.
3. Nonproperty assaultive crimes—aggravated assault, simple assault, and forcible rape—were negatively correlated with population density. These crimes do not involve the theft of property but do involve the threat or use of force.

After reporting these findings, we discovered the same pattern of relationships for these ten types of crimes when they were correlated with other variables representing the major structural characteristics of the twenty-six cities. These relationships are presented in table 4-1.

The pattern that emerges is clearly consistent with the classification scheme suggested. The direction of the correlation between victimization rates and each structural characteristic is the same within each of the three crime groupings for seventy-six of the eighty correlations in table 4-1. Each of the three nonproperty assaultive crimes, for example, is negatively correlated with population density, crowding, percentage foreign-born, and percentage on public assistance and is positively correlated with percentage white, median income, percentage unemployed, and percentage aged 12 to 24. The pattern for property crimes without contact is the same, except for motor-vehicle theft, which is positively correlated to both population density and percentage on public assistance. Regarding the direction of the correlations between the structural characteristics and victimization rates, the

Table 4-1
Zero-Order Correlations between Structural Characteristics of Cities and Ten Types of Crime

| | Property Crimes | | | | | | | Nonproperty Assaultive Crimes | | |
| | With Contact | | | Without Contact | | | | | | |
	Robbery with Injury	Robbery without Injury	Larceny with Contact	Burglary	Household Larceny	Larceny without Contact	Motor-Vehicle Theft	Rape	Aggravated Assault	Simple Assault
Density	.43*	.52*	.57*	-.64*	-.77*	-.64*	.19	-.48*	-.44*	-.41*
Crowding	-.32	-.17	.01	-.46*	-.48*	-.62*	-.31	-.49*	-.65*	-.77*
Percentage white	-.16	-.34	-.26	.38	.56*	.59*	.05	.34	.43*	.66*
Median Income	.16	.20	.01	.43*	.44*	.60*	.07	.30	.43*	.59*
Percentage unemployed	.28	.15	.06	.11	.01	.18	.31	.22	.15	.30
Percentage foreign-born	-.06	-.03	.17	-.40*	-.41*	-.39*	-.06	-.29	-.45*	-.31
Percentage on public assistance	.31	.19	.35	-.32	-.58*	-.57*	.26	-.22	-.41*	-.44*
Percentage aged 12-24	-.01	-.11	-.10	.45*	.52*	.53*	.13	.34	.34	.38

$*p < .05$; two-tailed test of significance.

pattern for property crimes with contact is different from the patterns of the other two groups of crimes. Robbery with injury, robbery without injury, and personal larceny with contact are all positively correlated to population density, median income, percentage unemployed, and percentage on public assistance. They are all negatively correlated to percentage of the population that is white and percentage of the population between the ages of 12 and 24 (although the last set of correlations is very low). The correlations of these three crimes with percentage foreign-born and with crowding are not consistent; robbery with and without injury are negatively correlated with these variables, while personal larceny with contact is positively correlated with them.

Table 4-2 presents our grounded classification more formally. It is clear that the classificiation has two underlying dimensions: victim-criminal contact and property or nonproperty offense. When these two dimensions are cross-classified, we note that only three cells have crimes from the NCS. The fourth cell—nonproperty, noncontact crimes—is empty. This may be because certain types of crimes systematically have been excluded from the survey questions. One of the questions on the NCS asks, for example, "Did anyone threaten to beat you up, or threaten you with a knife, gun, or some other weapon, *not* including telephone threats?" The survey question thus excluded responses that would fall in the fourth category—that is, telephone threats are a nonproperty, noncontact crime. Thus nonproperty, noncontact crimes, as well as victimless crimes, are not included in the NCS surveys and therefore cannot appear in our classification.

Some Applications of the Empirical Classification

The utility of our classification can be demonstrated using data from the NCS. First, we compare the zero-order correlations obtained using this classification with those obtained using the UCR categories of violent crimes (homicide, rape, robbery, and aggravated assault) and property crimes

Table 4-2
Typology of Criminal Victimization

	Contact Crimes	*Noncontact Crimes*
Property crimes	Personal larceny with contact	Personal larceny without contact
	Robbery with injury	Household burglary
	Robbery without injury	Household larceny
Nonproperty Crimes	Aggravated assault	Nonproperty
	Simple assault	Noncontact
	Rape	

(burglary, larceny, and motor-vehicle theft). This categorization of crimes has been used in a number of analyses of crime and victimization rates (for example, Harries 1976; Balkin 1979). Most often, the crime rates within each of these categories of crime are added together to obtain a crime-rate index—violent-crime rate and property-crime rate. The important point here is that the UCR classification combines both contact and noncontact property crimes into a single index—property crimes. As we have shown earlier, however, these two types of crimes have a very different relationship with the most important structural characteristics of cities. Furthermore, the UCR classification puts together robbery (a property crime with contact, according to our classification) and rape and assault (nonproperty assaultive crimes, according to our classification) into a single violent-crime index. The effect of combining crimes into a single index when the signs of the correlations of those crimes with important dependent variables (structural characteristics of cities) differ is to cover up important relationships that otherwise would be observed between those rates and the dependent variables. Piazza (1980) comments similarly on a situation involving attitude items and demographic variables. This covering up is seen in the results presented in table 4-3.

When these two UCR indexes are created (using the NCS data) and then correlated with population density across the twenty-six cities included in

Table 4-3
Comparison of Correlations between Population Density
and Crimes Combined According to the UCR Classification
and the Grounded Typology

	r	Statistical Significance[a]
UCR Classification		
Violent crimes	.12	NS
(rape, robbery, aggravated assault)		
Property crimes	− .52	.006
(burglary, larceny, motor-vehicle theft)		
Grounded typology		
Property crimes with contact	.59	.002
(robbery with injury, robbery without injury, personal larceny with contact, motor-vehicle theft)		
Property crimes without contact	− .74	.000
(burglary, household larceny, personal larceny without contact)		
Nonproperty assaultive crimes	− .47	.019
(rape, simple assault, aggravated assault)		

NS = not significant.
[a]Significance levels are for two-tailed tests of significance.

the NCS, violent crime has a correlation of .12 and property crime a correlation of $-.52$ (see table 4-3). When the crime rates within each of the categories of our classification are added together, higher correlations result. The correlations are .59 for property crimes with contact, $-.74$ for property crimes without contact, and $-.47$ for nonproperty assaultive crimes. At least for NCS data, researchers who use the traditional crime categories from the UCR will find generally lower zero-order correlations than those found using our categories. This occurs because the UCR categories combine crimes that, both empirically and theoretically, should be separate. This is perhaps most dramatically seen in the correlation between population density and the UCR violent-crimes classification. The UCR classification combines crimes that are related in empirically different ways to population density: rape ($r = -.48$), aggravated assault ($r = -.44$), robbery with injury ($r = .43$), and robbery without injury ($r = .52$). Similar results occur with other structural characteristics.

A further application of our crime categories to the NCS data may be instructive. In the next chapter, we discuss in more detail the negative relationship between property crimes without contact and population density. These crimes require that the victim and the criminal not come into contact; in low-density areas, this may be a result of a lower degree of community surveillance (see Reppetto 1974; Newman 1972). In addition, the rate of property crimes with contact may be greater in densely populated areas, where avoiding contact is more difficult. This suggests that densely populated cities should have relatively more property crimes involving contact than crimes not involving contact. To test this proposition, z-scores were calculated for property crimes with contact and property crimes without contact for each of the twenty-six central cities. A measure of the relative preponderance of contact crimes over noncontact property crimes was then formed by subtracting the z-scores for property crimes without contact from the z-scores for property crimes with contact. The correlation between this index and population density (.83) is in the expected direction, since, if the theory is correct, more contact property crimes than noncontact property crimes occur in densely populated areas.

Summary

We have discovered a three-category grounded classification of crimes, using survey data on the rates of criminal victimization. This classification shows a high degree of consistency in its relationships with eight important structural characteristics of cities. Furthermore, the three categories of our grounded classification produce higher correlations than the two-category classification of crimes that is often applied to data from the UCR. Finally, an index constructed from the relative difference in rates between property crimes with contact and property crimes without contact demonstrates further the utility of our grounded classification.

In the next chapter, we will use the three categories of crimes derived in this chapter to analyze the relationships between criminal victimization and the degree of density and crowding in the NCS sample cities.

5

Population Density, Crowding, and Criminal Victimization

Crime has long been associated with the rise of the city, and the process of urbanization has been isolated as one of the main factors responsible for fostering the social conditions that produce criminal behavior. (See chapter 2 for a review of the ecological approach to the study of crime.) For this reason, sociologists and criminologists often compare crime rates for urban and rural areas and conclude that most crime rates increase with increased urbanization (see Wolfgang 1968). The professional literature indicates that, even within urban areas, crime is concentrated in specific parts of cities rather than evenly distributed throughout the area. Specifically, the central parts of the cities, with the highest population densities, seem to have the highest crime rates (see Shaw and McKay 1969). It is in the central parts of cities that there are high concentrations of low-income groups, such as the elderly and minority citizens, and it is also in these areas that most of the criminal offenders and their victims reside (Wilson 1970). Most of the criminological literature has relied on the crime rates of cities as reported to the police, although it has been expected that other approaches, such as victimization surveys, would find the same general relationship between criminal behavior and urbanization.

These factors have led many researchers to argue that there is a positive zero-order relationship between the size of areas, and their population density, and crime rates (Wolfgang 1968; Mladenka and Hill 1976; Wirth 1938; Skogan 1977a; Wilson and Boland 1976; Hemley and McPheters 1974; Beasley and Antunes 1974). Population size and population density are sometimes used interchangeably (see Mayhew and Levinger, 1976). Since central cities of urban areas tend to be the largest in size and also tend to have the highest population density, their generally high crime rate is often claimed to be a result of these variables. In his review of nineteenth-century studies of urban ecology, Morris (1971), for example, states that one of the major points made in these studies is "the role of objective socio-economic factors such as poverty, education, density of population, and external value systems in determining and perpetuating criminal behavior" (p. 66).

Not all researchers have accepted the idea of a positive zero-order relationship between population density and crime rates, however. As early as the first part of the nineteenth century, Guerry (1833) tested the hypothesis: "Crime is due to population density"; on the basis of the available data in France, he rejected the hypothesis. Very recently, other researchers have begun to question the relationship between density and crime (Kvalseth 1977; Boland 1976). Kvalseth (1977) stated that in Atlanta, for example, population density

> . . . was among the most highly significant determinants of crime for the various types of crimes, with the exception of residential and non-residential burglaries. The effect of population density was in all significant cases a negative one. (p. 108)

With few exceptions, however, the hypothesis of the positive relationship between population density and crime rates lingers on. This may be due, in part, to Wirth's influence on the thinking of urban researchers. Wirth saw in large cities a breeding place for all types of social disorganization; greater density meant a decrease in primary controls and greater individualization, which led to the increase in secondary controls over behavior. This line of thought has exerted great influence over a large number of sociologists and criminologists.

Modern ecological studies attempt to answer a wide variety of research questions by (1) including various measures of physical and social characteristics (such as population density, crowding, unemployment rates, educational level, percentage white), (2) conducting analyses on many levels of aggregation (such as nations, regions, SMSAs, central cities, census tracts, blocks, and individuals), and (3) examining new sources of information on the incidence of crimes (such as self-report and victimization surveys).

The research reported in this chapter is in this tradition; that is, it is an ecological study of the relationship of population density (population per square mile and percentage of households with more than 1.01 persons per room) to victimization rates in twenty-six central cities. Such a study combines two research traditions: (1) the study of behavioral effects of population density on individuals and (2) the study of intercity variations in crime rates.

Previous Studies of Population Density and Crowding

Researchers have used measures of gross density as variables in studies that have used different levels of analysis. For McCarthy, Galle, and Zimmern (1975) defined density as "the number of persons per square mile," while Schmidt, Goldman, and Flimer (1979) used the number of people per census block. These measures of density are sometimes referred to as indicators of areal density (Kirmeyer 1978) or of external density (Baldassare 1979), and, since they are gross measures of density, they present some problems of interpretation. Carnahan, Guest, and Galle (1974) point out that an area of a city may have the same gross density as another area or city but for entirely different reasons:

> While one area has a low density because most of the land is for non-residential use, presumably business or industrial, another area has a low density because each structure has one dwelling unit and each structure has a large amount of surrounding area. (p. 490)

Because gross-density measures are indicators of the central tendencies in large areas, they obscure the possible variations in density that exist within these areas. Nevertheless, measures of gross density are useful for many purposes—for example, as indicators of the overall ability of an area or a city to support living organisms—and thus the importance of the concept is universally accepted (Baldassare 1979).

Because measures of external density are conceptually inappropriate for answering some kinds of research questions, researchers have also developed the concept of internal density (Baldassare 1979) or in-dwelling density (Kirmeyer 1978). Internal density refers to the number of persons per dwelling unit (such as the number of rooms or the square footage) in comparison to the number of people living in these small units of space. More specifically, the Bureau of the Census has applied the concept of residential crowding; that is, crowding exists when there are too many persons per room in a residence. Crowding is most often defined as a dwelling unit with 1.01 or more persons per room. This definition ignores important differences within dwelling units, such as the amount of square footage available, the amount of available space surrounding the dwelling unit, or the different space needs of the residents because of age or sex differences. Crowding is often thought to have "negative health, social, mental, and criminal consequences, because it creates a situation of too many contacts, too much stress, not enough privacy, too much stimulation, and too many interpersonal thwarthings" (Baldassare 1979, p. 19; see also Galle, Gove, and McPherson 1972; Gove and Hughes 1980).

We decided to use the term *internal density* rather than *crowding* to denote the percentage of households with 1.01 or more persons per room, because the term *crowding* is often used to describe "a negative perception of excessive density—a subjective experience of social overload" (Rapoport 1975, p. 8). This is certainly not what is measured by our indicator of internal density.

Studies of Variations in Intercity Crime Rates

A few research studies have dealt with intercity variations in crime or victimization rates and their relationships with internal and external density.

Harries (1974) compared 134 SMSAs on the basis of their 1970 social indicators, including density (population per square mile) and crowding (persons per room), and crime rates from the UCR. In his analysis, he found a positive relationship between metropolitan crime rates and both density and crowding. He also found a high negative relationship ($r = -.748$) between suburban population density and violent crime, which he suggests may be spurious because of regional differences.

McCarthy, Galle, and Zimmern (1975) examined the relationship between interpersonal violence (homicide and aggravated assault) and population density and crowding (internal density) in 171 American cities, using 1970 data. They found that crowding is strongly related to both homicide and assault, except in the South. They also found significant relationships for the multiple-partial correlation between density measures and interpersonal violence. The results were very similar for correlations based on 1950 data.

Booth, Welch, and Johnson (1976) used UCR data to examine the relationships between crowding (internal density) and crime rates and between dwelling unit or areal density (dwelling units per square mile) and crime rates in 656 cities. They found that crowding was related to crime rates, even after using controls, such as for region, race, education, income, age, population size, and nativity. They also found that, even though the amount of explained variance was not large, it was consistent for most crimes, lending support to the idea of a relationship between crowding and crime rates.

Freedman, Heska, and Levy (1975) examined the relationship between population density and crime rates in metropolitan areas of the United States. They found that about 9 percent of the variation in crime was associated with density; when other social factors were controlled, however, this relationship disappeared. They also noted that the relationship of violent crime to density is lower than that of property crime to density.

Galle, McCarthy, and Gove (1974) investigated the relationships between population density, household crowding (internal density), and pathology (alcoholism, homicide, suicide) in U.S. cities. They found no significant relationship between crowding and pathology, but density tended to be negatively related to suicide and homicide.

In an analysis of victimization-survey data from twenty-six central cities, Wilson and Boland (1976) found a positive relationship between population density and personal robbery (robberies in which ten dollars or more was taken). In research based on law-enforcement data from ten SMSAs, Spector (1975) reported no significant relationship between population density and the incidence of violent crime. In their study of the data from ninety-five SMSAs, Pressman and Carol (1971) found that the partial correlation between crime rates and population density indicated that there was a negative relationship between density and rates of murder, forcible rape, and aggravated assault, while the correlation with robbery was positive. These relationships were not statistically significant, however. In a study of 199 SMSAs, Greenwood and Wadycki (1973) found that the relationship between population density and both property and violent crimes was negative but not statistically significant.

This brief review indicates that studies examining the relationships of internal and external density to crime and victimization rates have been carried out at many different levels of aggregation. It is important to recognize that the relationships between citywide external density, internal density, and victimization rates may not be the same as those found at other levels, such as block level or census-tract level (see Alker 1969; Roncek 1975; Slatin 1969). The analysis of this data, however, allows us to investigate the relationships between two measures of density and rates of criminal victimization at one important level of social aggregation—the level of central cities. This is the level of much criminological theorizing (for example, Shaw and McKay 1969; Wirth 1938; Skogan 1977a). Furthermore, relationships at this level of analysis may help to shed some light on relationships at lower levels of aggregation (Gove and Hughes 1980).

Procedures

The study reported here focused on the relationship between population per square mile (external density) and the percentage of housing units with more than 1.01 persons per room (internal density) and measures of victimization rates for ten different crimes in twenty-six central cities. The victimization rates are again from the National Crime Surveys. (See appendix A for a description of the NCS research design and appendix B for the definitions of the ten different crimes.) As noted in chapter 3, there is reason to believe that the NCS data are more satisfactory than the UCR data in terms of probable validity. Therefore, we use these data in this chapter. The data on external and internal density for the twenty-six central cities were gathered by the U.S. Bureau of the Census (1976).

Some of the inconsistencies in the findings from studies examining the relationship of population density to crime rates are probably a result of treating different types of crimes as a unitary phenomenon. Therefore, we examined the zero-order relationship of both external and internal density to each of the ten victimization rates recorded in the NCS: robbery with injury, robbery without injury, personal larceny with contact, personal larceny without contact, household burglary, household larceny, aggravated assault, simple assault, rape, and motor-vehicle theft. These ten crime rates were then regressed on both external and internal density. Only then did we combine crimes into indexes of property crimes with contact (robbery with injury, robbery without injury, and personal larceny with contact); property crimes without contact (burglary, household larceny, and personal larceny without contact); and nonproperty assaultive crimes (aggravated assault, simple assault, and rape). Each of these indices is a summative index of the z-scores for the relevant crimes.

Findings

The zero-order correlations presented in table 5-1 show some consistent patterns. In the crimes that we label nonproperty assaultive crimes, both internal and external density are negatively correlated to each victimization rate in a statistically significant manner. For those crimes that we label property crimes with contact, only external density is significantly correlated. In this case, each relationship is positive; that is, the greater the population per square mile, the greater the rate of victimization for the three property crimes with contact. The third group of crimes—property crimes without contact—shows correlations with both internal and external density that

Table 5-1
Zero-Order Correlations between Internal and External Density and Victimization Rates

	External Density	Internal Density
Property crimes with contact		
Robbery with injury	.42*	−.32
Robbery without injury	.52**	−.17
Personal larceny with contact	.57**	.01
Property crimes with contact index	.56**	−.18
Property crimes without contact		
Household burglary	−.64***	−.46*
Household larceny	−.77***	−.48*
Personal larceny without contact	−.64***	−.62***
Motor-vehicle theft	.19	−.31
Property crimes without contact index[a]	−.73***	−.56**
Nonproperty assaultive crimes		
Aggravated assault	−.44*	−.65***
Simple assault	−.40*	−.77***
Rape	−.48*	−.49*
Nonproperty assaultive crimes index	−.50**	−.72***

[a]This index does not include motor-vehicle theft.
  * $p < .05$; two-tailed test.
 ** $p < .01$; two-tailed test.
*** $p < .001$; two-tailed test.

are statistically significant and negative in all cases, except for motor-vehicle theft. Some of these significant relationships are large ($R^2 > .50$). It is also important that internal and external density are not highly correlated. Thus, they are ideally suited for independent variables in multiple-regression analysis.

The multiple-regression analyses (table 5-2) indicate that our measures of internal and external density account for a large percentage of the inter-city variation in nonproperty assaultive crimes. The adjusted R^2 for rape is .38; for aggravated assault, .53; and for simple assault, .67. When a summative index of nonproperty assaultive crimes is formed by adding together the z-scores for these three crimes for each city, the adjusted R^2 for this index, regressed on internal and external density, is .68 ($p < .001$). The zero-order correlations between this index and internal and external density are $-.72$ ($p < .001$) and $-.50$ ($p < .01$), respectively. This analysis indicates that, on the aggregate level, nonproperty assaultive crimes tend to be highly and negatively correlated with internal and external density.

The second group of crimes, property crimes with contact, includes three offenses: robbery without injury, robbery with injury, and personal

Table 5-2
Proportions of Intercity Variations in Victimization Rates Accounted For by Internal and External Density

	Adjusted R^2
Property crimes with contact	
Robbery with injury	.26*
Robbery without injury	.26*
Personal larceny with contact	.27*
Property crimes with contact index	.32**
Property crimes without contact	
Household burglary	.52***
Household larceny	.74***
Personal larceny without contact	.70***
Motor-vehicle theft	.07
Property crimes without contact index[a]	.75***
Nonproperty assaultive crimes	
Aggravated assault	.53***
Simple assault	.67***
Rape	.38**
Nonproperty assaultive crimes index	.68***

[a]This index does not include motor-vehicle theft.
  * $p < .05$; two-tailed test.
 ** $p < .01$; two-tailed test.
*** $p < .001$; two-tailed test.

larceny with contact. The adjusted R^2 for robbery both with and without injury is .26; for personal larceny, .27. The summative index for these three crimes has an adjusted R^2 of .32 ($p < .01$) when regressed on internal and external density. As might be expected from an examination of the zero-order correlations in table 5-1, this relationship is due to external density. Internal density does not add significantly to the variance accounted for by external density.

The third group of crimes, property crimes without contact, are personal larceny without contact, burglary, household larceny, and motor-vehicle theft. The adjusted R^2 for personal larceny without contact is .70; for burglary, .52; for household larceny, .74; and for motor-vehicle theft, .07. For the composite index of property crimes without contact (not including motor-vehicle theft), the R^2 for the regression of this index on internal and external density is .75. Here, both internal and external density are negatively related to property crimes without contact. The zero-order correlations are $-.56$ and $-.73$, respectively.

Discussion

The findings in this chapter are interesting from several perspectives. Perhaps the most important finding is that density has at least two independent dimensions (note that the correlation between internal and external density is only .10) that are significantly related to victimization rates. Although it would be useful to include a measure of perceived density to compare with our measures of internal and external density, this comparison is not possible because data on perceived density are unavailable. In this respect, however, it should be noted that Gove, Hughes, and Galle (1979) found that number of persons per room is strongly related to the subjective experience of crowding.

These patterns of relationships between our measures of density and the victimization rates are complex, but this complexity is understandable when our typology of criminal victimization is used. First, both property crimes without contact and nonproperty contact crimes are negatively related to both internal and external density. This finding is contrary to a large volume of criminological and sociological literature, which leads to an expectation of a positive relationship between density and victimization. Since two distinct measures of density produce negative correlations with rates of victimization, it appears that theories that predict a positive relationship between density and crime rates at the city level should be reexamined.

This finding might also cause researchers to rethink the relationship between density and criminal activity at lower levels of aggregation. A step in that direction has recently been made by Cohen and Felson (1979) and

Cohen, Felson, and Land (1980). Especially relevant to the findings given here is their concept of guardians. The lack of effective guardians (people who are able to prevent violations from occurring either by their physical presence alone or by some form of direct action) is assumed to increase the likelihood of direct-contact predatory property crimes.

Second, property crimes with contact do not show the same negative relationship with our measures of density. Although internal density shows no significant relationship with these victimization rates, there is a positive relationship with our measure of external density. The positive relationship is consistent with (1) the opportunity explanation—"the denser the population, the more frequent and easily a robber can find a victim"—or (2) the subculture explanation—"dense cities should . . . make it easier for like-minded individuals to find and associate with each other under conditions of weak communal control and so, by their interacting, intensify any proclivities they may have for criminal activity" (Wilson and Boland 1976, pp. 223-224).

Which of these theories or explanations are useful at the individual level is a question that has not been addressed by this study. It may be that each of these factors is important and that the weight of each varies with the type of victimization involved. These are important questions for future research.

In the next chapter, we examine the relationship between law-enforcement manpower and the rate of criminal victimization. This examination is placed within the framework of environmental-control theory, with the number of police per capita and the population per square mile considered as factors in reducing the likelihood of crime.

6 Law-Enforcement Manpower and Criminal Victimization

With the publication of the results from the LEAA-sponsored surveys of criminal victimization in twenty-six large American central cities, there was a renewed interest in the correlates of crime in urban areas (for example, Booth, Johnson, and Choldin 1977; Decker 1978; Nelson 1978; Skogan, 1977a). These studies included demographic, economic disorganizational, and social-control variables in order to account for differences in crime rates among cities. In this chapter, we employ an environmental-control perspective, which suggests that certain aspects of the environment can deter criminal activities. This perspective is consistent with some suggestions of Jeffrey (1971), who states, among others, the basic assumptions of behaviorism and environmentalism:

> The human being is regarded as an input-output system capable of receiving messages from and responding to the environment. . . . Adaptation of the organism to the environment is the key process. Behavior is viewed as the means by which the organism adapts to an environmental system. (p. 167)

Specifically, we will investigate the relationship between two indicators of environmental control (the number of police per capita and population density) and the rates of criminal victimization in twenty-six large American cities. Our rationale for selecting these two variables as indicators of environmental crime control is as follows.

Our first indicator of environmental control is the number of police per capita. The function of law-enforcement officers is peacekeeping and the prevention and detection of criminal violations. It is not unreasonable to expect that the greater the number of police per capita, the greater their potential control of criminal activities. Our second indicator of environmental control is population per square mile (density of population). As the number of police per capita is expected to have a controlling effect on the amount of criminal activity, we expect that the number of people in a given area will also have a controlling effect on the amount of criminal activity.

Our hypothesis concerning the number of police per capita is common-sensical. One of the first suggested responses to crime problems is to hire more police officers. The President's Commission on Law Enforcement and Administration of Justice (1967) has stated: "There is impressive evidence that in many cities there are too few policemen" (p. 106). At the same time, there is no conclusive evidence concerning the relationship between the number of police per capita and the incidence of criminal behavior. For example, the President's Commission (1967) also concluded: "There appears to be no correlation between the differing concentrations of police and the amount of crime committed, or the percentage of known crimes solved, in the various cities" (p. 106). Harries (1976) found a positive relationship between the number of police per capita and crime indicators, and argues that this is so because a high crime rate leads to greater expenditure for police protection. Boggs (1965), however, concludes that the visibility of police could either increase or decrease the amount of known crime:

> The presence of police also plays an unknown part in crime occurrence. The more police in an area, the more crimes can be observed. Conversely, the presence of police might be a deterrent, so that fewer crimes occur. (p. 903)

Similarly, Chapman (1971) has noted that the visible presence of police is intended to have a controlling effect on criminal activity:

> Patrol is supposed to cause the potential offender to believe that there is no reasonable opportunity available to violate the law successfully. This is the concept of deterence. Basic to the concept is the assumption that to increase the threat of apprehension raises the risk in committing the crime and so reduces the likelihood of the crime being committed. (p. 78)

Our second hypothesis—that population density is negatively related to criminal victimization—is consistent with the suggestions of some urban planners (Jacobs 1961), who have advocated land use that would provide circulation on streets at all times in order to reduce crime. Angel (1968) identified critical-intensity zones—areas where potential victims come into contact with potential offenders and there are too few people in the area to provide effective surveillance. These are critical-intensity zones as compared with areas outside these zones, which are characterized as having either too few or too many people—too few to provide enough victims or too many so that the risk of offensive behavior is too great.

It may seem obvious that a lack of victims can deter criminal behavior. Some social researchers, such as Wolfgang and Ferracuti (1967) and Curtis (1975), have argued for a positive relationship between population density and crime, particularly because of the strong positive association between population density and poverty areas in large cities. Others have argued that cities create situations of overcrowding, which lead people to act in an antisocial manner (Calhoun 1963; Lorenz 1967; van den Berghe 1974). Still others have predicted a positive relationship between population density and crime because of the increased opportunities for criminal behavior in cities (Harries 1974; Hage 1972).

Procedures

Most research on the relationship between environmental factors and criminal behavior has relied on reported crime. The research described in this chapter relies on victimization rates rather than on reported rates, which allows us to avoid such problems as increases in reported crime due to larger numbers of police (see Boggs 1965). The decision to use victimization data rather than reported crime rates also is based partly on the fact that victimization data seem to be more accurate than reported crime rates (see chapter 3).

In order to assess the relationship between our indicators of environmental control and crime rates in central cities, we used data from three sources. Our data on number of police per capita is from the U.S. Department of Justice (1974), and our measure of population density is from the U.S. Bureau of the Census (1976).[1] Data on crime rates were drawn from the National Crime Surveys. (See appendix A for a description of the NCS research design and appendix B for the definitions of the ten different crimes.)

Although some studies have investigated the relationship between the crime rate and the number of police per capita (Skogan 1977a; Harries 1976; Swimmer 1974) or between the crime rate and population density (Skogan 1977a; Harries 1974; Weathersby 1970; Greenwood and Wadycki 1973), they have often defined the crime rate in terms of a summative index of several different types of crimes. Our approach in this chapter is similar to that of Mayhew and Levinger (1976) and Boland (1976), in that we differentiate between different types of crimes. We focus on the relationship of two indicators of environmental control and victimization rates for ten different types of crimes: robbery with injury, robbery without injury, personal larceny with contact, personal larceny without contact, household burglary, household larceny, aggravated assault, simple assault, rape, and motor-vehicle theft. It is important that these different types of crime not be treated as a unitary phenomenon. To ascertain the relationship between each of these offenses and our indicators of environmental control for the twenty-six cities, we correlated the number of police per capita and population density with each victimization rate. In addition, we calculated partial-correlation coefficients for the relationship of population density, controlling for the number of police per capita, and the reverse, for each type of victimization.

Findings

The relationships between the number of police per capita, population density, and the ten types of victimization rates form a definite pattern. In table 6-1, we note that seventeen of the possible twenty correlations are statistically significant at the .05 level or beyond. The positive and negative signs of the relationships differ according to the nature of the offense. These relationships are consistent with the classification of crimes developed in chapter 4.

1. Nonproperty assaultive crimes (aggravated assault, simple assault, and forcible rape) are negatively correlated with both the number of police per capita and population density. These crimes do not involve the theft of property but do involve the threat or use of force.
2. Property crimes without contact (household burglary, household larceny, and personal larceny without contact) are negatively correlated with both the number of police per capita and population density. These are all property crimes in which the offender and the victim typically are not in direct contact. Another property crime without contact—motor-vehicle theft—is not significantly correlated with either population density or the number of police per capita.
3. Property crimes with contact (robbery with injury, robbery without injury, and personal larceny with contact) are all positively correlated with both the number of police per capita and population density, although the correlation between the number of police per capita and robbery with injury is not statistically significant. These are all property crimes that bring the offender and the victim into direct contact.

The zero-order correlation between density and the number of police per capita is positive and very strong ($r = .63$). This indicates, as might be expected, that cities that have a higher population density also have a higher number of police per capita. We therefore calculated the partial correlations between each victimization rate and population density, controlling for the number of police per capita. For the same reason, we calculated partial correlations between each victimization rate and the number of police per capita, controlling for population density. These partial correlations are presented in table 6-2. As in table 6-1, a definite pattern emerges. When controlling for the number of police per capita, population density is negatively related to property crimes without contact (with the exception of motor-vehicle theft) and positively related to nonproperty assaultive crimes. When controlling for population density, the number of police per capita is negatively related to property crimes without contact (albeit weakly), negatively related to nonproperty assaultive crimes (somewhat more strongly), and not significantly related to property crimes with contact.

Discussion

Our examination of the relationship between two indicators of environmental control and criminal-victimization rates shows that crime cannot be

Table 6-1
Zero-Order Correlations between the Number of Police per Capita,
Population Density, and Ten Types of Offenses

	Number of Police per Capita	Population Density
Property crimes with contact		
Robbery with injury	.19	.43**
Robbery without injury	.39**	.52***
Personal larceny with contact	.40**	.57***
Property crimes without contact		
Household burglary	−.58****	−.64****
Household larceny	−.67****	−.77****
Personal larceny without contact	−.62****	−.64****
Motor-vehicle theft	−.01	.19
Nonproperty assaultive crimes		
Aggravated assault	−.48***	−.44***
Simple assault	−.56****	−.41**
Rape	−.62****	−.48***

  * $p < .10$
 ** $p < .05$
*** $p < .01$
**** $p < .001$

treated as a unitary phenomenon. The analysis indicates that the relationship between victimization rates and both the number of police per capita and population density is dependent on the type of offense involved.

Contrary to a considerable volume of literature, which suggests a positive relationship between population density and crime rates (Beasley and Antunes 1974; Hemley and McPheters, 1974; Mayhew and Levinger, 1976; Shaw and McKay 1969; Skogan 1977a; Wilson and Boland 1976; Wirth 1938; Wolfgang 1968), we find that the zero-order correlations between victimization rates and population density are dependent on the type of offense involved. Population density is negatively related to property crimes without contact and nonproperty assaultive crimes and positively related to property crimes with contact; that is, the greater the population density, the lower the rate of victimization by property crimes without contact and nonproperty assaultive crimes and the greater the rate of victimization by property crimes with contact. This is an unexpected finding, as discussed in chapter 5. We will focus on the relationship of population density, controlling for the number of police per capita and criminal victimization. Consistent with our hypothesis—which suggests that, the greater the population density, the greater the environmental control—we find that, controlling for the number of police per capita, population density is negatively related to property crimes without contact (with the exception of motor-vehicle theft). This finding is consistent with Reppetto's (1974)

Table 6-2
Partial Correlations between the Number of Police per Capita, Population Density, and Ten Types of Offenses

	Number of Police per Capita (controlling for population density)	Population Density: (controlling for number of police per capita)
Property crimes with contact		
Robbery with injury	−.11	.40**
Robbery without injury	.09	.39*
Personal larceny with contact	.06	.45**
Property crimes without contact		
Household burglary	−.31	−.43**
Household larceny	−.37*	−.60****
Personal larceny without contact	−.36*	−.41**
Motor-vehicle theft	−.17	.26
Nonproperty assaultive crimes		
Aggravated assault	−.29	−.21
Simple assault	−.43**	−.09
Rape	−.46**	−.16

    * $p < .10$
   ** $p < .05$
  *** $p < .01$
 **** $p < .001$

discussion of household burglary, in which he notes that burglars seek out neighborhoods that are isolated and in which they feel inconspicuous.

Contrary to our second hypothesis, however, population density is positively related to property crimes with contact. Several tentative explanations might be offered for this relationship. First, it is consistent with the views of some researchers, who interpret population density as an indication of crowding (Calhoun 1963; van den Berghe 1964), or of increased opportunities for crime (Boggs 1965; Mayhew and Levinger 1976; Booth, Welch, and Johnson 1976). Second, one could argue that, as population density increases, environmental control also increases, which makes it more difficult to commit crimes without contact. If it is difficult to commit personal larceny without being seen, for example, the offender may have to make contact with the victim; if burglarizing a home without being seen is difficult, the offender may resort to robbery—or what was intended as burglary may become a robbery (Reppetto 1974; U.S. Department of Justice 1976a; 1976b).[2]

Finally, although all three nonproperty assaultive crimes are negatively related to population density (as hypothesized), none of these relationships is statistically significant.

Our analysis shows definite zero-order relationships between the number of police per capita and the rate of criminal victimization; the direction of the relationship, however, depends on the type of victimization involved. The number of police per capita is negatively related to property crimes without contact (with the exception of motor-vehicle theft), negatively related to nonproperty assaultive crimes; and positively related to property crimes with contact (with the exception of robbery with injury). This pattern of results may help explain the ambiguity, mentioned in the introduction to this chapter, concerning the relationship between the number of police per capita and crime rates—that is, the relationship is positive or negative depending on the type of crime. As mentioned earlier, our analysis is based on victimization surveys rather than on reported crime, which prevents the observed relationships from being contaminated by the fact that, with more police, more crimes can be observed.

The partial correlations between the number of police per capita (controlling for population density) and victimization rates are negatively related to property crimes without contact. The negative relationship supports our hypothesis that increased environmental control is associated with decreases in property crimes without contact. Once again, this is consistent with Repetto's (1974) study of residential burglary.

The partial correlations between the number of police per capita and nonproperty assaultive crimes are negative. This is also consistent with our original hypothesis.

Finally, the number of police per capita (controlling for population density) is not related to the rate of property crimes with contact. This finding might suggest that the number of police per capita is not a deterrent for these types of crimes. We must be cautious, however, in drawing this type of conclusion.

Although the results are generally consistent with our original hypotheses, it is important to mention some limitations of the results presented in this chapter. The first is that the analysis is based on central cities rather than on smaller units, such as census tracts or neighborhoods. Thus, it is impossible for us to make a causal statement, since the burglary rates in high-density cities might be lower because environmental control is greater or because these cities have relatively low rates of burglary in their low-density areas (that is, an ecological fallacy). Second, we have examined the two best available indicators of environmental control (population density and the number of police per capita) because we have only a limited number of cases—twenty-six central cities—which makes examination of a larger number of independent variables likely to lead to "chance fitting of the data" (Cohen and Cohen 1975). Third, we are aware of the problems involved in calculating first-order partial-correlation coefficients when the three variables are highly intercorrelated. See Gordon (1968) for an excellent discussion of this problem. There is a danger that the differences between partial correlations will be much larger than the differences between zero-order correlations.[3] It should be noted, however, that the pattern of the relative strengths and sizes of the partial-correlation coefficients in each of the three categories of our typology of offenses is remarkably stable for the partial correlation coefficients presented in table 6-2.

Summary

This chapter attempted to shed some light on the relationships between the rates of criminal victimization and certain urban characteristics in twenty-six large central cities. We investigated indicators of the effects of environmental control in the urban setting on the rates of criminal victimization. Two indicators of environmental control were employed: number of police per capita and population density.

It was also assumed that various types of criminal victimization might be differently related to our indicators of environmental control. The types of victimization included property crimes with contact, property crimes without contact, and nonproperty assaultive crimes. Both indicators of environmental control were negatively related to property crimes without contact and nonproperty assaultive crimes.

Finally, the number of police per capita (controlling for population density) is associated with lower rates of victimization for both property crimes without contact and nonproperty assaultive crimes. The number of police per capita does not appear to be related to property crimes with contact, however. This finding suggests the possibility that increasing the size of police departments may be effective in reducing the rate of certain types of criminal offenses. The nature of the data used in this study, however—that is, cross-sectional, aggregate-level data—makes any policy implications drawn from this chapter very tentative.

In the next two chapters, the relationships between the urban structural characteristics described in chapter 2 and the victimization rates for two separate age groups (juveniles and the elderly) are examined. In these two chapters, we urge the reader to consider the cautions outlined in chapter 2 regarding the limited number of cities involved in the NCS and the use of a large number of independent variables. For that reason, we consider the analyses in the next two chapters exploratory.

Notes

1. We actually employ data on the number of full-time-equivalent police personnel per 100,000 citizens. These figures are from *Expenditure*

and *Employment Data for the Criminal Justice System* (U.S. Department of Justice 1974).

2. For example, if members of the household surprised a burglar in their home and then were threatened or harmed by the intruder, the act would be classified as assault. If the intruder were to demand or take cash and/or property from the household members, the event would be classified as robbery (U.S. Department of Justice 1976*a*; 1976*b*).

3. The zero-order correlation between household larceny and the number of police per capita, for example, is $-.67$, while household larceny correlates $-.77$ with population density. The first-order partial correlations between the number of police per capita (controlling for population density) and population density (controlling for the number of police per capita) with household larceny, however, are $-.37$ and $-.60$, respectively. The differences between zero-order correlations are magnified in the first-order partial correlations. This problem is exacerbated by the possibility of a high degree of sampling error in a study based on only twenty-six cases.

**Patterns of
Juvenile Victimization**

An increasing volume of criminological literature deals with juvenile delinquency and its correlates. Very little attention has been paid, however, to the problem of the criminal victimization of juveniles, with the exception of the recent upsurge of interest in child abuse (Bakan 1972; Chase 1975). There is also an interest in juvenile victimization in the school setting (Hepburn and Monti 1979; U.S. Department of Health, Education and Welfare 1977). The relatively limited volume of work on this subject warrants more interest, however, because victimization surveys show that juveniles consistently report the highest rates of victimization among all age groups. There has been a great deal of concern among researchers, criminal-justice personnel, and law-enforcement agencies regarding the criminal victimization of other age groups. The victimization of the elderly has received special attention, partly because of the great amount of fear of victimization expressed by older people (see Goldsmith and Goldsmith 1976; also see chapter 8 in this book).

Lalli and Savitz (1976) found, however, that there are also high levels of fear of victimization among juveniles. A few articles reported some preliminary findings on juvenile victimization (Feyerherm and Hindelang 1974; Friedman, Mann, and Adelman 1976). Because of the high rates of victimization, as well as the apparent fear, it seems appropriate to focus deeper attention on the subject of juvenile victimization.

To a certain extent, crime appears to be age-specific; that is, the arrest rates and the victimization rates of age groups are parallel. Empey (1978), for example, points out that the victimization rate for personal crimes (rape, robbery, assault, and larceny) decreases with each older age group after adolescence, just as the arrest rates do. The pattern for violent crimes is different, however, for juveniles. They are the ones most likely to be victimized by violent crimes, even though they do not have the highest arrest rate for these crimes; thus, the correlates of crime rates and victimization rates for juveniles are not necessarily the same.

Some research has investigated the relationship between the urban structure and the types and rates of juvenile delinquency. The Chicago school, for example, has delineated the spatial concentration of juvenile delinquency in specific parts of large urban areas (Shaw and McKay 1969). Most criminal offenders and their victims reside in those parts of urban areas where there is a high concentration of low-income groups, such as the elderly and ethnic minorities (Wilson 1970). Therefore, a comparative study of the urban characteristics associated with juvenile victimization (as opposed to juvenile crime rates) would seem to be an appropriate starting point in this neglected area of study. In this chapter, we investigate the relationship between juvenile victimization and the urban structural characteristics described in chapter 2.

Procedures

The focus of this chapter is on the relationships among several urban structural characteristics and the NCS rates for juveniles (aged 12 to 19) in twenty-six large American central cities.[1] (See appendix A for a description of the NCS research design.) The independent variables for the study are population density (population per square mile), percentage of the population between 12 and 19 years of age, percentage white, percentage foreign-born, percentage unemployed, percentage on public assistance, percentage blue-collar, and a summative index based on the median income and education for each city—a socioeconomic index (SEI).[2]

Stepwise multiple regression is used to assess the relationship of each structural characteristic to the rate of juvenile victimization. This procedure enters the independent variables in a stepwise fashion: the first variable entering the equation accounts for the greatest amount of variance in the dependent variable; the second independent variable entering the equation accounts for the greatest amount of variance in the dependent variable that is not accounted for by the first independent variable; the third independent variable entering the equation accounts for the greatest amount of variance unaccounted for by the first two independent variables; and so on. In this way, we are able to evaluate whether or not each new variable entering the regression equation accounts for additional (unaccounted for) variance in the dependent variable. Our strategy is to regress each victimization rate (dependent variable) on the urban structural characteristics (independent variables) for all twenty-six cities. We then assess the statistical significance of the additional contribution of each new independent variable, using an F-test.[3]

Findings

In this section, we present the results of the stepwise multiple regressions for each of three categories of victimization (property crimes without contact, property crimes with contact, and nonproperty assaultive crimes). Each analysis is based on the victimization rates (dependent variables) for twenty-six central cities. These rates are regressed on the urban structural characteristics mentioned earlier.

Table 7-1 presents the result of our stepwise multiple regression for juvenile victimization by property crimes without contact. The most consistent result is that density is the first variable to enter each of these equations. The proportion of intercity variation accounted for by density ranges from 64 percent for household larceny to 21 percent for motor-vehicle theft. The relationship between density and the rates of household larceny, burglary, and personal larceny without contact are statistically significant at the .001 level. The relationship between density and motor-vehicle theft is significant at the .05 level. Each of these property crimes without contact is negatively correlated to population density; that is, cities that are less densely populated tend to have a higher rate of juvenile victimization for these four crimes. Another important urban structural characteristic accounting for intercity variation is the percentage of white population in the city. This variable is positively correlated to both household larceny and personal larceny without contact. The percentage of white population accounts for

Table 7-1
Stepwise Regression for Property Crimes without Contact

	R^2	Change in R^2	F-Value for Change in R^2	Zero-Order r
Dependent variable: household burglary				
Density	.42	.42	17.54****	−.65
Dependent variable: household larceny				
Density	.64	.64	42.96****	−.80
Percentage white	.76	.12	11.56***	.50
Dependent variable: motor-vehicle theft				
Density	.21	.21	6.20**	−.45
SEI	.32	.11	3.69*	.42
Dependent variable: personal larceny without contact				
Density	.52	.52	26.21****	−.72
Percentage white	.75	.23	21.21****	.61
SEI	.84	.09	11.89***	.60
Percentage foreign-born	.87	.03	4.47**	−.36

Note: This table includes only the independent variables that are significantly related to juvenile victimization ($p < .10$).

*Change in R^2 is significant at the .10 level.
**Change in R^2 is significant at the .05 level.
***Change in R^2 is significant at the .01 level.
****Change in R^2 is significant at the .001 level.

an additional 12 percent of the variation in household larceny ($p < .01$) and an additional 23 percent of the variation in personal larceny without contact ($p < .001$).

An additional variable that has some explanatory value is SEI (the summative index based on the median and education for each city). It contributes an additional 9 percent to the explained variance in personal larceny without contact ($p < .01$) and an additional 11 percent to the explained variance in motor-vehicle theft ($p > .05$ but $p < .10$). This variable is positively correlated to both of these rates. The final structural characteristic that adds significantly to the explained variance of these victimization rates is the percentage of foreign-born people in the city. This variable adds 3 percent to the explained variance in personal larceny without contact ($p < .05$).

The urban structural characteristics employed in our analysis account for an unusually large proportion of the variation in victimizations by household larceny and personal larceny without contact. Four urban structural characteristics account for 87 percent of the variation in juvenile victimization by personal larceny without contact, while two structural characteristics account for 76 percent of the variation in household larceny victimization.

Table 7-2 presents the results of our stepwise analysis for nonproperty assaultive crimes (rape, simple assault, and aggravated assault). The most consistent finding for these rates of juvenile victimization is that the percentage white in urban areas is the first variable to enter each of the stepwise-regression equations. The proportion of intercity variation accounted for by percentage white varies from 22 percent for rape and aggravated assault ($p < .05$) to 41 percent for simple assault ($p < .001$). The relationship between percentage white and juvenile victimization is positive for each type of crime; that is, cities with a higher percentage of white population tend to have a higher rate of juvenile victimization by nonproperty assaultive crimes.

Another important structural characteristic that accounts for additional variation in these victimization rates is the percentage of the urban population that is foreign-born. This structural characteristic contributes 28 percent to the variation accounted for in juvenile victimization by aggravated assault ($p < .01$), 17 percent to the variation accounted for in victimization by simple assault ($p < .01$), and 11 percent to the variation in victimization by forcible rape ($p < .10$). The relationship between the percentage foreign-born and these victimization rates is negative; that is, cities with a higher percentage foreign-born tend to have lower rates of victimization for these crimes.

Percentage unemployed adds significantly to the explained variance of two types of victimization—forcible rape and simple assault. It adds 11 percent to the variance accounted for in simple assault ($p < .05$) and 10 percent

Table 7-2
Stepwise Regression for Nonproperty Assaultive Crimes

	R^2	Change in R^2	F-Value for Change in R^2	Zero-Order r
Dependent variable: *rape*				
Percentage white	.22	.22	6.64**	.47
Percentage unemployed	.31	.09	3.23*	.33
Percentage foreign-born	.42	.11	4.08*	−.21
Percentage aged 12-19	.50	.08	3.34*	−.20
Dependent variable: *aggravated assault*				
Percentage white	.22	.22	6.67**	.47
Percentage foreign-born	.49	.28	12.48***	−.44
Dependent variable: *simple assault*				
Percentage white	.41	.41	16.61****	.64
Percentage foreign-born	.58	.17	9.54***	−.31
Percentage unemployed	.69	.11	7.45**	.31
Percentage blue-collar	.73	.04	3.07	−.33

Note: This table includes only the independent variables that are significantly related to juvenile victimization ($p < .10$).
*Change in R^2 is significant at the .10 level.
**Change in R^2 is significant at the .05 level.
***Change in R^2 is significant at the .01 level.
****Change in R^2 is significant at the .001 level.

to the variance accounted for in forcible rape ($p < .10$). For both these types of victimization, the greater the percentage unemployed, the greater the victimization rate. Two other variables contributed modestly to the explained variance, but neither was statistically significant at the .05 level. These variables are the percentage blue-collar and the percentage of the population between 12 and 19 years of age, both of which are negatively correlated with juvenile victimization.

In our analysis, we find that 73 percent of the intercity variation in juvenile victimization by simple assault is accounted for by four structural characteristics of urban areas (percentage white, percentage foreign-born, percentage unemployed, and percentage blue-collar). In the case of juvenile victimization by forcible rape, 50 percent of the variance is explained by four structural characteristics (percentage white, percentage unemployed, percentage foreign-born, and percentage of population in the 12-19 age group). Finally, in the case of juvenile victimization by aggravated assault, two urban structural variables account for 49 percent of the variance (percentage white and percentage foreign-born).

The stepwise-regression analysis for property crimes with contact (personal larceny with contact, robbery without injury, and robbery with injury) indicates that the structural characteristics of cities used in our analysis are not very useful in accounting for variance in these crimes. The only structural characteristic that enters any of the equations for these three crimes is SEI, which accounts for only 16 percent of the intercity variation in personal larceny without contact.

Discussion

In examining the structural characteristics that account for intercity variation in the victimization rates of juveniles for property crimes without contact, we note the consistently high negative relationship between density and each of these crimes ($-.80$ to $-.45$). The fact that the relationship between victimization rates and density is negative is especially interesting in light of the supposedly positive relationship between crime and density (see Shaw and McKay 1969; Wolfgang 1968; Mladenka and Hill 1976; Wirth 1938; Wilson and Boland 1976).[4] Given that the data we are analyzing are on the city level of analysis, it is not possible to provide a definitive explanation of this relationship. We might speculate, however, that, in cities that are more densely populated, it is more difficult to commit property crimes without contact because of an increase in visibility under the condition of high density. This fact has been noted by Cunningham (1976) and Reppetto (1974). Cunningham (1976) states that the burglar "actively attempts to avoid human contact. He is thus more than usually sensitive to evidence of occupancy, of being observed and possibly reported out of suspicion, and being surprised in the process of his crime" (pp. 47-48). Contrary to the opportunity theory mentioned in chapter 5, the availability of a potentially large number of victims does not necessarily indicate an increased victimization rate for property crimes.

A consistent pattern also emerges from the analysis of the structural characteristics that account for intercity variations in nonproperty assaultive crimes. For all three of these crimes (simple assault, aggravated assault, and rape) the percentage white and the percentage foreign-born enter the equations. In each case, the higher the percentage of the population that is white and the lower the percentage that is foreign-born, the higher the rates of victimization are.

Although this pattern is consistent for all three types of nonproperty assaultive crimes, our explanation of the pattern has remained very tentative. First, what constitutes an assaultive crime is problematic, especially for juveniles. Sellin and Wolfgang (1964) note that street fights, domestic quarrels, and scuffles at schools are often considered by juveniles to be assaults, even though they are not considered to be felonious assault. In addition, in the case of juvenile victimization, the retrospective definition of attacker and victim may be based more on the result of the fight (that is, the winner is the attacker and the loser is the victim) than on the circumstances leading to the confrontation. Second, although these results might indicate that whites and non-foreign-born have higher rates of nonproperty-assaultive victimization, this is clearly not the case. The 1976 victimization survey (U.S. Department of Justice, 1976c) indicates, for example, that the victimization rate (per thousand) by rape was .7 for whites and 1.9 for blacks; the victimization rate by assault was 24.9 for whites and 28.9 for blacks. Thus, we see that blacks have a higher victimization rate for these crimes than whites. The problem is that the analysis is conducted at the city level. The relationship between the percentage of the population that is white and the rate of nonproperty assaultive crimes indicates only that cities with higher percentages of white citizens tend to have higher rates of victimization by nonproperty assaultive crimes. Third, one might even speculate that the higher percentage of whites provides a larger pool of victims for nonwhite criminals. This argument is contradicted by a number of studies that indicate that nonproperty assaultive crimes tend to be intraracial rather than inter-racial (see Amir 1971; Curtis 1975; Wolfgang 1958).

Summary

In this chapter, we examined the urban structural characteristics associated with intercity variation in juvenile victimization rates. This is a relatively neglected area of research, since much of the literature has dealt with juveniles as offenders rather than as victims and has not attempted to account for intercity variation in victimization rates. In the analysis, we discovered a strong negative relationship between motor-vehicle theft, household larceny, and household burglary and population density (also see chapter 5). We have suggested that this may be a result of the increased visibility that occurs under the condition of high population density.

Although we have not been able to provide a satisfactory explanation of the pattern of intercity variation for nonproperty assaultive victimization of juveniles, the pattern of intercity variation is clear—victimization tends to be greater in cities with higher percentages of white population and lower percentages of foreign-born population.

The stepwise approach used in this chapter uncovered strong relationships between urban structural characteristics (independent variables) and juvenile victimization by property crimes without contact and by nonproperty assaultive crimes. This approach has been less useful, however, in accounting for property crimes with contact. Given the cautions outlined in chapter 2 regarding the limited number of cities involved in the NCS and the large number of potential independent variables, further investigations of the patterns discovered are needed. Reasons for the differences in the effect of the structural variables on the different types of crime should also be explored.

Notes

1. In order to examine victimization rates for the 12-19 age group for robbery with injury, robbery without injury, aggravated assault, simple assault, personal larceny with contact, and personal larceny without contact, it was necessary to combine the victimization rates for the 12-15 and 16-19 age groups. This was accomplished by multiplying the number of residents in each of the two age groups by the rate for that age group and adding these products together. This sum was then divided by the sum of the total numbers in each of the age groups.

2. Our measure of socioeconomic conditions was based on both the median income and the median education for each city. The correlation for these two variables was .71. Our measure of socioeconomic conditions (SEI) was obtained by computing the z-scores for median income and median education and then summing these z-scores for each city.

3. The F-test we use is one recommended by Cohen and Cohen (1975, p. 107).

4. Several researchers, however, have found a negative relationship between population density and victimization rates (Kvalseth 1975, 1977; Boland 1976; Shichor, Decker, and O'Brien 1979).

Household Victimization of the Elderly

It has been assumed for some time that older people in the United States frequently are the victims of criminal acts—perhaps the most frequently victimized group in the nation (Butler 1975; Butler and Lewis 1977; Cook and Cook 1976). It has been argued that the aged frequently are victimized because of their vulnerability; that is, they are less able to ward off criminal attackers, they very often live in the high-crime areas of the large urban areas, and so on (U.S. House of Representatives 1977). Even though crime reports from a few scattered areas did not indicate that the aged were greatly victimized, it was believed that the aged might be more frequently victimized than police reports indicated. It was thought, for example, that the aged might be less likely than younger people to report instances of victimization because of fear of retaliation, inability to engage the attention of the police, lack of knowledge of where to go to report crimes, or lack of confidence in the criminal-justice system (Butler 1975). Today, criminologists and gerontologists agree that the American aged are not a highly victimized group and that younger age groups are more likely to be criminally victimized (U.S. Department of Justice 1977). The acceptance of this view is the result of national victimization surveys that were conducted for the Law Enforcement Assistance Administration (LEAA) by the U.S. Bureau of the Census (U.S. Department of Justice 1975, 1976a, 1976b). The significance of the problem of criminal victimization of the aged is not entirely a question of victimization rates, however (Decker 1980; Gubrium 1974).

Three factors intensify criminal victimization as a problem for the aged. First, the aged are more fearful of criminal victimization than are younger age groups, even though they are victimized less. Several researchers have noted this distinction between the actual rates of victimization and the fear of victimization (U.S. House of Representatives 1977; Young Rifai 1976). Furthermore, the age group that shows the highest levels of fear is the older residents in densely populated urban areas (Clemente and Kleinman 1976; Labowitz 1975; Sundeen and Mathieu 1976). Indicative of this relationship between fear and urban areas is the conclusion of Clemente and Kleinman (1976):

> The aged residents of cities over 50,000 show significantly greater fear of crime than either their younger counterparts or older inhabitants of suburbs, small towns, and rural areas. (p. 210).

73

Older people's fear of criminal victimization is due, in part, to the generally higher rates of fear among women and the fact that the sex ratio of the aged favors women (Clemente and Kleinman 1976). It is known that the aged spend more time watching television than younger age groups do (Hendricks and Hendricks 1977), and it is possible that the violence depicted through the mass media may serve to heighten older people's fear of criminal victimization.

A second intensifying factor in the victimization of the elderly is the differential impact of a criminal act. The aged are, in general, a low-income group, and thus even a relatively small monetary loss can have a large impact on the older person. Cunningham (1976) found in Kansas City, for example, that nearly half of the elderly victims had an annual income of less than $3,000. Since the income level of many of the victimized aged is so low, the impact of a criminal act may be greater than it would be for a younger person. The physical consequences of a criminal act involving bodily harm might also be more severe for the aged victim than for a younger person.

A third factor that intensifies the impact of victimization of the aged is the location of violent crimes. The aged are more likely to be victimized in or near their homes than are younger age groups (Antunes et al. 1977). In Kansas City, Cunningham (1976) found that over 80 percent of the serious crimes committed against the aged were in or near their homes. The location of the criminal victimization of the aged is important because it is evident that the aged are not voluntarily placing themselves in situations of high risk but that many of the crimes are being committed in or near their homes. They obviously cannot avoid the places in which they are being victimized, which means that they are not capable of reducing their risk through avoidance. In addition, some older people report that they are fearful of leaving their homes, thus essentially placing themselves under house arrest. In this situation, because of their fear, the aged are victims whether or not they are ever actually criminally victimized. Young Rifai (1976) found that fear of victimization could cause significant behavioral changes among older persons. Of the crimes that are of greatest concern to the older population, none is more important in terms of actual rates of victimization and fear of crime than household victimization. For the crimes included in the national victimization surveys (U.S. Department of Justice 1977), three-fourths of the victimizations reported by the elderly involve household larceny or household burglary. This figure is higher than comparable figures for any other age groups (see table 8-1). In addition, Reppetto (1974) has indicated that household crimes can be the most threatening because they violate a person's sense of privacy and the feeling of safety in the sanctuary of the home. Our approach to the study of criminal victimization of the aged is to analyze the differential rates of household victimization of the aged in different cities, in an attempt to determine whether some characteristics of urban areas are associated with the rates of victimization.

Table 8-1
Victimizations Reported on the NCS and Classified as Household
Victimizations, by Age Groups

Age Group	Percentage of Victimizations Classified as Household Victimizations
12-19	63
20-34	59
35-49	67
50-64	67
65 +	75

Source: Based on data reported by the U.S. Department of Justice (1977, tables 4 and 9).

Procedures

This chapter focuses on the relationships between several urban structural characteristics and NCS household-victimization rates for the elderly in twenty-six large U.S. central cities. Household victimization includes household burglary—that is, unlawful or forcible entry (or attempted entry) into a home—and household larceny—that is, the theft (or attempted theft) of property or cash from a home or its immediate vicinity that did not involve forcible or unlawful entry.[1] (See appendix A for a description of the NCS research design.)

The independent variables we use in the study are population density (population per square mile), percentage elderly (percentage of the population over 65 years of age), percentage between 12 and 24 years of age, percentage white, percentage unemployed, percentage on public assistance (percentage of families receiving public assistance), and percentage blue-collar. Since median income and median education are closely related, both theoretically and statistically ($r = .71$ for these twenty-six cities), we combined these measures into a single index of socioeconomic conditions (SEC). Specifically, our SEC measure was obtained by computing the z-scores for median income and median education and then summing these z-scores for each city. Data on the independent variables came from the 1970 census (U.S. Bureau of the Census 1976).

Stepwise multiple regression is used to assess the relationship of each of the structural characteristics to the rate of household victimization. This procedure enters the independent variables in a stepwise fashion. The first variable entering the equation accounts for the greatest amount of variance in the dependent variable; the second independent variable entering the equation accounts for the greatest amount of variance in the dependent variable that is not accounted for by the first independent variable; the third independent variable entering the equation accounts for the greatest amount of variance unaccounted for by the first two independent variables; and so on.

In this way, we are able to evaluate whether or not each new variable entering the regression equation accounts for additional (unaccounted for) variance in the dependent variable. Our strategy is to regress the victimization rates (dependent variable) on the urban structural characteristics (independent variables) for all twenty-six cities. We then assess the statistical significance of the additional contribution of each new independent variable using an F-test (Cohen and Cohen 1975).

Findings

The intercity variation in household victimization rates is well accounted for by differences in structural characteristics of cities. Three structural characteristics account for 61.5 percent of the variation in victimization rates for burglary (see table 8-2). Density contributes the most to the explained variance (36.8 percent). The zero-order correlation (r_{xy}) is -.61, indicating that less-dense cities have higher victimization rates for burglary.

The next two most important factors explaining additional variance have to do with the socioeconomic conditions (SEC) of the city. A combination of the median education and median income for cities, SEC adds 14.7 percent to the explained variance, while the percentage on public assistance adds an additional 10 percent. The zero-order correlation between each of these variables and burglary indicates that cities that are better off tend to have higher rates of household burglary. These three variables each account for a significant amount of variance $(p < .05)$ in household burglary when they are added to the equation. None of the other structural characteristics in our analysis account for a significant amount of additional variance in household burglary.

Table 8-2
Stepwise Regression for Household Burglary of the Elderly, Regressed on Structural Characteristics of Central Cities

Independent Variables	Total R^2	Change in R^2	F-Value for Change in R^2	Zero-Order Correlation
Density	.368	.368	13.95**	−.61
SEC	.515	.147	6.97*	.50
Percentage on public assistance	.615	.100	5.72*	−.17

*Change in R^2 is significant at the .05 level.
**Change in R^2 is significant at the .01 level.

Household larceny is also strongly correlated with density (see table 8-3). Density alone accounts for 61.8 percent of the intercity variation. Again, density is negatively correlated with the rate of victimization. The next two factors that enter the equation are the percentage blue-collar, which accounts for an additional 12 percent of the variation, and SEC, which accounts for an additional 4.6 percent of the variance. Once again, socioeconomic factors are important in explaining the rate of household victimization. All three variables (density, percentage blue-collar, and SEC) are significant at the .05 level when they enter the equation predicting household larceny. None of the other structural characteristics account for a significant amount of the variation in the rate of household larceny.

There is a pattern for both types of household victimization of the elderly in the central cities of large urban areas. The first variable to enter each equation is density, which is negatively correlated with rates of victimization. This indicates that less-dense areas have higher rates of victimization. This finding is not consistent with the traditional criminological explanation (suggesting a positive relationship between crime rates and population density), which has probably focused more on violent crimes than on property crimes. These results are consistent, however, with the findings of Boland (1976), Kvalseth (1977), and those reported in chapter 5, which indicate a negative relationship between density and crime rates for selected types of crimes for the total population. This finding has not been reported for household victimizations among the aged.

It is very possible that the negative relationship between density and the rate of household victimization is linked to the fact that less-dense areas provide better settings for the criminal offenders, in that they are less visible or conspicuous in these areas. Cunningham (1976) states, for example, that the burglar "actively attempts to avoid human contact. He is thus more than usually sensitive to evidence of occupancy, of being observed and possibly reported out of suspicion, and being surprised in the process of his

Table 8-3
Stepwise Regression for Household Larceny of the Elderly, Regressed on Structural Characteristics of Central Cities

Independent Variables	Total R^2	Change in R^2	F-Value for Change in R^2	Zero-Order Correlation
Density	.618	.618	38.89***	−.79
Percentage blue-collar	.739	.120	10.57**	−.25
SEC	.784	.046	4.66*	.46

*Change in R^2 is significant at the .05 level.
**Change in R^2 is significant at the .01 level.
***Change in R^2 is significant at the .001 level.

crime" (pp. 47-48). In interviews with adjudicated burglars, Reppetto (1974) notes that they actively seek out neighborhoods that are isolated and in which they feel inconspicuous. Finally, Angel (1968) identifies critical-intensity zones—areas in which possible victims attract possible offenders but where too few people are present to provide effective surveillance.

The next two variables that enter each of the equations for household victimization can be viewed as indicators of relative affluence. For burglary, SEC is positively correlated and the percentage on public assistance is negatively correlated to the rate of burglary. This indicates that more affluent areas (controlling for density) have higher rates of burglary. For household larceny, SEC is again positively correlated to the victimization rate, while percentage blue-collar is negatively correlated. Once again, more affluent areas (controlling for density) have higher rates of household victimization of the elderly. This finding supports Reppetto's (1974) notion "that high residential crime rate will correlate with characteristics that . . . attract residential criminals" (p. 33).

Summary

In conclusion, our study has shown that a few urban structural characteristics account for a high proportion of the intercity variation in the rates of household victimization among the elderly. Three variables (density, SEC, and percentage on public assistance) account for almost 62 percent of the variance in household burglary rates, and three variables (density, SEC, and percentage blue-collar) account for more than 78 percent of the variance in household larceny. The pattern of results for both types of household victimization of the elderly indicates that cities that are less densely populated and have higher levels of affluence have the highest rates of household victimization.

Although we find the results presented in this chapter interesting and sometimes surprising, it must be remembered that they are on an aggregate level of analysis (city level). They describe the relationship between the rate of household victimization of the elderly in central cities and the structural characteristics of those cities. Research should be extended in an attempt to discover if the pattern of results remains the same at different levels of analysis, such as census areas within cities or neighborhoods.

Note

1. In the NCS, household victimizations also include motor-vehicle theft, since its rate is computed on a per household basis. Here we focus on household burglary and larceny.

Research and Social-Policy Implications

Validity of UCR and NCS Data

A number of important implications for future research can be drawn from the preceding chapters. In chapter three, we reported important differences between the UCR and NCS measures of the crime rate across the twenty-six cities included in the NCS. Although the crime-rate measures for motor-vehicle theft, burglary (residential and commercial combined), and robbery from the UCR and NCS showed enough agreement to suggest that they might be measuring the same underlying variables, those for other crimes showed little, if any, agreement. In fact, for aggravated assault, the relationship between the UCR and NCS measure was negative ($r = -.39$) for these twenty-six cities; that is, cities rated high on aggravated assault according to one of these measures tended to rate low according to the other. Something is clearly wrong with one or both of these two measures of aggravated assault.

From the studies and data reviewed in chapter 3, we conclude that the NCS measures are probably more valid than the UCR measures for most crimes. This has important implications for studies that rely on official statistics for measures of the crime rate—the majority of intercity studies (not to mention intracity, interstate, and international studies). This is especially crucial when the variable of interest is aggravated assault, rape, or personal larceny.

Classification of Crimes

There has been a long-standing tradition of classifying crimes in various ways. One of the most popular classifications is that used in the UCR—classifying crimes as violent crimes (homicide, rape, robbery, and aggravated assault) and property crimes (burglary, larceny, and motor-vehicle theft). Our studies of the NCS data (see, especially, chapters 4 and 5) have led to an empirically based classification of crimes as property crimes with contact (robbery with injury, robbery without injury, and personal larceny with contact), property crimes without contact (household larceny, burglary, and personal larceny without contact), and nonproperty assaultive crimes (aggravated assault, simple assault, and rape).

Combining crimes into a single index from two or more of these categories can substantially reduce the relationships between the index and other variables. Combining property crimes with and without contact (which correlate in opposite directions with most of the structural characteristics we examined) into a single category to form a property-crime index clearly goes against the rules of index construction. The empirical result is to reduce two substantial relationships (one positive and the other negative) to a single, nearly null relationship.

Researchers should be very cautious when combining crimes into a single index. This caution should include examining not only the interrelationships among the separate crime rates but also the parallelisms of the relationships between the crime-rate measures and other variables.

Density and Crowding

It is important to distinguish between different variables not only in the area of crime rates but also in the area of population density. In chapter 5, we showed that external density (population per square mile) and internal density (percentage of the households with 1.01 or more persons per room) are related in different ways to the ten crime rates we examined. In addition, when both density measures are used in a multiple-regression equation, they account for a substantial percentage of the intercity variation in crime rates.

The findings reported in chapter 5 do not support the generally held belief that population density and crime rates are positively associated for cities—that is, that densely populated cities have high crime rates. In fact, such a belief is supported only for the relationship between population per square mile and property crimes with contact. This suggests a reexamination and rethinking of the relationship between density and crime.

Limitations Resulting from Sample Size

An important limitation on researchers using the NCS is that the data are limited to twenty-six central cities. This data base is unlikely to expand in the near future, partly because of funding limitations. Furthermore, although it was reasonable in this study to use data collected in a two-year period in a single cross-sectional study, it would not be reasonable to combine data from a ten-year or longer period. In fact, the types of data analyzed here on a city level probably will not be collected again in the foreseeable future.

Throughout this book, we have been explicit in our concern about the use of multivariate analyses with only twenty-six cases. Rather than using multiple-regression analyses with numerous independent variables, we have looked for compelling and suggestive patterns in the data (the only exceptions are chapters 7 and 8). Population per square mile, for example, shows statistically significant correlation ($p < .05$, $n = 26$) with nine of the ten crimes reported in the NCS; for five of these ten crimes, the correlation is significant beyond the .01 level, and for three of the ten, it is statistically significant beyond the .001 level. This result is not easily explained away by claiming that there are too few cases to support this sort of analysis. Furthermore, there is a convincing pattern to these relationships; that is, they correlate similarly within our three-category classification of crime. This classification, in turn, is supported not only by the zero-order correlations of population density with crime rates in each category but by the correlations of several other structural characteristics of cities. Again, it is the consistency of these patterns that adds support for our conclusions. Future research using these data must avoid the shotgun approach of using every possible independent variable to explain intercity variation in crime rates.

Social-Policy Implications

Given the limitations of having only twenty-six cases and a central-city-level analysis, any policy implications drawn from our studies must be tentative. In chapter 6, for example, we reported that the number of police per capita (controlling for population density) is associated with lower rates of victimization for both property crimes without contact and nonproperty assaultive crimes, while the number of police per capita does not appear to be related to property crimes with contact. This finding suggests the possibility that increasing the size of police departments may be effective in reducing the rate of certain types of criminal offenses. Given that we are not able to control for the effects of a large number of other possibly relevant independent variables, however, this conclusion must remain tentative.

The most obvious and most important implication for policymakers is that they should not assume that all types of crimes can be approached with a single, monolithic criminal-justice policy. Instead, the development of criminal-justice policy should take into account the particular type of crime. In addition, our analyses indicate that policies should consider the relationships between population density and crowding and these different types of crime. Although it is tempting to assume that the crime rate is positively associated with these two variables, our findings indicate that the relationship between them and different crime rates is more complex.

Appendix A:
NCS Survey Design

The National Crime Surveys were conducted in twenty-six major cities to measure the extent to which residents aged 12 years and over, households, and places of business were victimized by selected crimes—completed or attempted—that are of major concern to the general public. For crimes committed against persons, the offenses were rape, robbery, assault, and personal larceny; for households, they were burglary, larceny, and motor-vehicle theft; and for commercial establishments, they were robbery and burglary. A description of the crimes appears in appendix B.

In this book, we analyzed data on the victimization rates gathered for twenty-six cities, corresponding roughly to calendar years 1973 or 1974. Specifically, for eight of the cities we examine, victimizations are reported for the period between April 1, 1974, and May 31, 1975 (Atlanta, Baltimore, Cleveland, Dallas, Denver, Newark, Portland, and St. Louis); for five of the cities, the period corresponds roughly to the calendar year 1974 (Chicago, Detroit, Los Angeles, New York, and Philadelphia); and, for thirteen of the cities, the period corresponds roughly to the calendar year 1973 (Boston, Buffalo, Cincinnati, Houston, Miami, Milwaukee, Minneapolis, New Orleans, Oakland, Pittsburgh, San Diego, San Francisco, and Washington, D.C.).

The basic frames from which the samples were drawn for the household surveys in each of the cities were the complete housing inventories of the 1970 Census of Population and Housing. To select a sample, each of the city's housing units was distributed among 105 strata on the basis of various characteristics. To account for residential housing units built after the 1970 census, a sample was drawn of permits issued for the construction of new buildings within each of the cities. This enabled the proper representation in the surveys of people occupying housing built since 1970.

On the average, slightly more than 10,300 of the approximately 12,000 households initially sampled in each city were found to be qualified for the interview (the others were found to be vacant, demolished, temporarily occupied by nonresidents, and so forth). The response rate for the households that qualified for interviewing was 96.5 percent. Thus, approximately 10,000 households were interviewed in each city, and more than 21,000 individuals from those households were interviewed. The final victimization rates were based on a complex weighting scheme designed to make the estimated victimization rates representative of the population of the city's households (for household crimes) and residents 12 years of age and over (for personal crimes).

For the survey of commercial establishments, the eligible geographic units were selected on the basis of field surveys. The units contained at least four but no more than six commercial establishments. On the average, slightly more than 2,830 were initially selected for inclusion in the sample, but almost 800 of these were found to be out of business at the time of the survey, no longer operating at the designated address, or otherwise un-qualified to participate. Of the commerical establishments that were eligible for participation, 98.2 percent participated in the interviews, for an average of almost 2,000 per city.

Further details of the survey design can be found in publications of the U.S. Department of Justice (1975, 1976*a*, 1976*b*).

Appendix B:
Definitions of Crimes
Used in the NCS
and the UCR

NCS Definitions

Assault: An unlawful physical attack, whether aggravated or simple, upon a person. Includes attempted assaults with or without a weapon. Excludes rape and attempted rape, as well as attacks involving theft or attempted theft, which are classified as robbery.

> *Aggravated assault:* Attack with a weapon resulting in any injury and attack without a weapon resulting either in serious injury (such as broken bones, loss of teeth, internal injuries, loss of consciousness) or in undetermined injury requiring two or more days of hospitalization. Also includes attempted assault with a weapon.

> *Simple assault:* Attack without a weapon resulting either in minor injury (such as bruises, black eyes, cuts, scratches, swelling) or in undetermined injury requiring less than two days of hospitalization. Also includes attempted assault without a weapon.

Burglary: Unlawful or forcible entry of a residence or business, usually, but not necessarily, attended by theft. Includes attempted forcible entry.

Larceny: Theft or attempted theft of property or cash without force. A basic distinction is made between personal larceny and household larceny.

> *Personal larceny with contact:* Theft of purse, wallet, or cash by stealth directly from the person of the victim, but without force or the threat of force. Also includes attempted purse snatching.

> *Personal larceny without contact:* Theft or attempted theft, without direct contact between victim and offender, of property or cash from any place other than the victim's home or its immediate vicinity. In rare cases, the victim sees the offender during the commission of the act.

> *Household larceny:* Theft or attempted theft of property or cash from a residence or its immediate vicinity. Forcible entry, attempted forcible entry, or unlawful entry are not involved.

Motor-vehicle theft: Stealing or unauthorized taking of a motor vehicle, including attempts at such acts. Motor vehicles include automobiles, trucks, motorcycles, and any other motorized vehicles legally allowed on public roads and highways.

Rape: Carnal knowledge through the use of force or the threat of force, including attempts. Statutory rape (without force) is excluded. Includes both heterosexual and homosexual rape.

Robbery: Theft or attempted theft, directly from a person or a business, of property or cash by force or threat of force, with or without a weapon.

> *Robbery with injury:* Theft or attempted theft from a person, accompanied by an attack, either with or without a weapon, resulting in injury. An injury is classified as resulting from a serious assault if a weapon was used in the commission of the crime or, if not, when the extent of the injury was either serious (such as broken bones, loss of teeth, internal injuries, loss of consciousness) or undetermined but requiring two or more days of hospitalization. An injury is classified as resulting from a minor assault when the extent of the injury was minor (such as bruises, black eyes, cuts, scratches, swelling) or undetermined but requiring less than two days of hospitalization.

> *Robbery without injury:* Theft or attempted theft from a person, accompanied by force or the threat of force, either with or without a weapon, but not resulting in injury.

Commercial crimes: Burglary or robbery of business establishments and certain other organizations, such as those engaged in religious, political, or cultural activities. Includes both completed and attempted acts.

Household crimes: Burglary or larceny of a residence or motor-vehicle theft. Includes both completed and attempted acts. Households consist of the occupants of separate living quarters meeting either of the following criteria: (1) persons, whether present or temporarily absent, whose usual place of residence is the housing unit in question or (2) persons staying in the housing unit who have no usual place of residence elsewhere.

Personal crimes: Rape, robbery of persons, assault, personal larceny with contact, or personal larceny without contact. Includes both completed and attempted acts.

UCR Definitions

Aggravated assault: Assault with intent to kill or for the purpose of inflicting severe bodily injury by shooting, cutting, stabbing, maiming, poisoning, scalding, or by the use of acids, explosives, or other means. Excludes simple assaults.

Burglary (breaking and entering): Burglary, housebreaking, safecracking, or breaking or unlawful entry of a structure with the intent to commit a felony or a theft. Includes attempted forcible entry.

Forcible rape: The carnal knowledge of a female, forcibly and against her will, in the categories of rape by force, assault to rape, and attempted rape. Excludes statutory offenses (no force used—victim under age of consent).

Larceny-theft (except motor-vehicle theft): The unlawful taking, carrying, leading, or riding away of property from the possession or constructive possession of another. Thefts of bicycles, automobile accessories, shoplifting, pocket-picking, or any stealing of property or article that is not taken by force and violence or by fraud. Excludes embezzlement, confidence games, forgery, worthless checks, and the like.

Motor-vehicle theft: Unlawful taking or stealing or attempted theft of a motor vehicle. A motor vehicle is a self-propelled vehicle that travels on the surface but not on rails. Specifically excluded from this category are motor boats, construction equipment, airplanes, and farming equipment.

Robbery: Stealing or taking anything of value from the care, custody, or control of a person by force or by violence or by putting in fear, such as strong-arm robbery, stickups, armed robbery, assaults to rob, and attempts to rob.

**Appendix C:
NCS and UCR Rates and
Structural Characteristics of
Twenty-six Central Cities**

Urban Structure and Victimization

Appendix C:
NCS and UCR Rates and Structural Characteristics of Twenty-six Central Cities

City		NCS Rates per Thousand Residential Population Aged 12 and Over					
	Rape	Aggravated Assault	Simple Assault	Robbery with Injury	Robbery without Injury	Personal Larceny with Contact	Personal Larceny without Contact
Atlanta	2	12	11	4	13	9	84
Baltimore	3	21	21	11	24	19	86
Boston	2	17	18	9	22	26	93
Buffalo	2	14	17	5	11	7	67
Chicago	2	16	14	7	22	17	74
Cincinnati	2	22	25	6	9	7	104
Cleveland	7	20	17	8	19	9	76
Dallas	2	18	17	3	9	6	110
Denver	3	23	27	6	13	6	128
Detroit	2	21	18	9	28	8	83
Houston	3	17	16	4	13	6	116
Los Angeles	2	17	22	5	13	8	112
Miami	1	7	5	3	6	5	39
Milwaukee	2	17	24	6	12	7	96
Minneapolis	4	18	28	7	14	6	113
New Orleans	3	13	13	5	13	14	80
Newark	2	8	6	8	16	11	35
New York	1	9	10	6	18	15	51
Oakland	3	16	18	7	15	10	92
Philadelphia	1	14	13	6	15	12	72
Pittsburgh	2	13	17	6	9	7	76
Portland	4	22	30	6	10	6	137
St Louis	1	14	14	5	14	9	83
San Diego	2	16	24	4	7	5	136
San Francisco	3	14	25	9	20	23	106
Washington, D.C.	1	6	7	5	13	12	53

Appendix C: *(continued)*

City	NCS Rates per Thousand Households			NCS Rates per Thousand Residential Population Aged 12 and Over		
	Household Burglary	*Household Larceny*	*Motor-Vehicle Theft*	*Combined Residential and Commercial Robberies*	*Combined Residential and Commercial Burglaries*	*Combined Personal Larcenies*
Atlanta	158	117	24	25.15	105.46	93
Baltimore	118	124	42	40.68	71.51	105
Boston	149	87	86	39.49	108.92	119
Buffalo	97	92	30	17.32	64.01	74
Chicago	122	86	38	35.08	67.45	91
Cincinnati	143	103	25	19.00	118.03	111
Cleveland	137	106	73	33.07	82.58	85
Dallas	161	178	23	16.43	105.83	117
Denver	166	187	40	23.79	105.82	134
Detroit	154	107	70	45.86	90.12	91
Houston	164	167	32	19.66	95.70	122
Los Angeles	149	145	39	22.00	89.74	120
Miami	85	66	18	18.53	68.46	44
Milwaukee	152	128	29	17.43	82.85	103
Minneapolis	177	164	41	22.63	111.88	120
New Orleans	112	116	32	23.12	72.19	94
Newark	98	49	40	29.06	67.17	45
New York	77	46	28	34.32	63.16	65
Oakland	174	108	36	30.75	142.47	102
Philadelphia	91	83	36	26.31	61.41	85
Pittsburgh	93	90	43	16.71	56.90	83
Portland	174	189	37	21.20	115.82	143
St. Louis	135	94	46	26.54	83.78	92
San Diego	138	190	25	11.62	79.12	141
San Francisco	115	85	38	33.14	84.40	129
Washington, D.C.	75	51	15	19.78	55.44	65

Appendix C *(continued)*

UCR Rates per Thousand Residential Population Aged 12 and Over

City	Rape	Aggravated Assault	Robbery	Larceny	Burglary	Motor-Vehicle Theft
Atlanta	1.33	10.21	13.20	58.55	50.92	12.47
Baltimore	.71	9.37	14.99	45.32	27.59	13.53
Boston	.85	4.97	13.54	27.44	31.16	40.84
Buffalo	.59	2.18	5.95	30.00	17.63	13.90
Chicago	.77	5.33	10.55	46.28	20.45	14.29
Cincinnati	.63	2.28	4.32	42.20	32.19	8.18
Cleveland	.86	5.34	11.96	31.32	25.03	26.69
Dallas	1.00	5.81	4.97	66.78	41.43	9.61
Denver	.98	4.66	5.60	47.34	41.60	15.52
Detroit	1.18	6.54	18.97	39.76	39.75	24.04
Houston	.60	2.06	6.77	35.57	30.74	13.00
Los Angeles	.89	6.51	6.15	39.16	30.41	14.07
Miami	.33	11.41	9.04	47.00	36.29	10.42
Milwaukee	.33	1.37	2.03	33.05	10.53	9.78
Minneapolis	.74	3.88	6.06	45.32	33.69	14.42
New Orleans	.57	4.85	7.15	33.22	21.76	14.98
Newark	1.08	8.01	15.97	34.94	38.20	24.67
New York	.66	6.68	12.67	26.52	25.74	11.99
Oakland	.86	7.21	12.21	66.42	57.35	18.35
Philadelphia	.54	3.57	6.86	18.45	14.52	11.45
Pittsburgh	.72	4.82	6.91	20.34	18.24	17.30
Portland	.84	5.77	6.06	64.31	42.07	13.14
St. Louis	1.09	8.38	13.02	69.88	48.86	21.42
San Diego	.32	2.04	2.62	49.24	21.35	8.35
San Francisco	.99	4.85	8.82	45.20	28.13	17.10
Washington, D.C.	1.17	7.03	14.05	44.86	23.12	9.23

Appendix C *(continued)*

City	Density[a]	Crowding[b]	Percentage White	Median Income ($)	Structural Characteristics				Number of Police per Million Population
					Percentage Unemployed	Percentage Foreign-Born	Percentage on Public Assistance	Percentage Aged 12-24	
Atlanta	3,779	11	48	8,410	3	1	9	13	4,246
Baltimore	11,568	8	53	8,815	4	3	10	12	4,814
Boston	13,963	7	82	9,133	5	13	14	14	4,084
Buffalo	11,205	7	79	9,133	5	8	9	12	3,579
Chicago	15,126	10	66	10,242	4	11	7	12	4,776
Cincinnati	5,794	9	72	8,894	4	3	8	12	8,894
Cleveland	9,893	7	61	9,109	5	8	9	12	3,861
Dallas	3,179	9	74	10,019	3	2	5	12	3,214
Denver	5,406	5	89	9,654	4	4	7	13	3,372
Detroit	10,953	7	56	10,045	7	8	8	12	4,400
Houston	2,841	10	73	9,876	3	3	4	13	2,174
Los Angeles	6,073	8	77	10,535	7	15	10	11	3,719
Miami	9,763	21	77	7,304	4	42	13	10	3,105
Milwaukee	7,548	7	84	10,262	4	6	6	12	3,363
Minneapolis	7,884	4	94	9,960	4	5	8	13	2,476
New Orleans	3,011	14	55	7,445	6	3	11	13	2,953
Newark	16,273	14	44	7,735	6	11	19	12	4,845
New York	26,343	10	77	9,426	4	18	10	11	5,585
Oakland	6,771	7	59	9,626	8	9	14	12	2,627
Philadelphia	15,164	6	66	9,366	5	7	9	11	5,422
Pittsburgh	9,422	6	79	8,800	5	6	9	12	3,173
Portland	4,294	3	92	9,794	8	6	5	12	2,468
St. Louis	10,167	12	59	8,182	7	3	10	12	5,276
San Diego	2,199	7	89	10,166	6	8	7	15	1,757
San Francisco	15,764	7	71	10,503	7	22	9	11	3,760
Washington, D.C.	12,321	12	28	9,580	4	4	7	13	8,354

[a]Population per square mile.
[b]Percentage of households with 1.01 or more persons per room.

Bibliography

Alker, H.R., Jr. 1969. "A Typology of Ecological Fallacies." In *Qualitative Analysis in the Social Sciences*, ed. M. Dogan and S. Rokkan, pp. 69-86. Cambridge, Mass.: MIT Press.

Althauser, R.P. 1974. "Inferring Validity from the Multitrait-Multimethod Matrix: Another Assessment." In *Sociological Methodology 1973-1974*. ed. H.L. Costner, San Francisco: Jossey-Bass.

Althauser, R.P., and Heberlein, T.A. 1970. "Validity and the Multitrait-Multimethod Matrix," in *Sociological Methodology*. ed. E.F. Borgotta and G. Bohrnstedt, pp. 151-169. San Francisco: Jossey-Bass.

Amir, M. 1971. *Patterns of Forcible Rape*. Chicago: University of Chicago Press.

Angel, S. 1968. "Discouraging Crime Through City Planning." University of California Institute of Urban and Regional Development, Center for Planning and Development Research, Working Paper No. 75, pp. 16-28.

Antunes, G.E.; Cook, F.L.; Cook, T.D.; and Skogan, W.G. 1977. "Patterns of Personal Crimes Against the Elderly." *Gerontologist* 17 (4):321-327.

Ardrey, R. 1966. *The Territorial Imperative*. New York: Atheneum.

Bailey, L.; Moore, T.F.; and Bailar, B.A. 1978. "An Interviewer Variance Study of the National Crime Survey Cities Sample." *Journal of the American Statistical Association* 73 (March):16-23.

Bakan, D. 1972. *Slaughter of the Innocents*. Boston: Beacon Press.

Baldassare, M. 1979. *Residential Crowding in Urban America*. Berkeley-Los Angeles: University of California Press.

Balkin, S. 1979. "Victimization Rates, Safety and Fear of Crime." *Social Problems* 26:343-358.

Barnes, H.E., and Teeters, N.K. 1959. *New Horizons in Criminology*. Englewood-Cliffs, N.J.: Prentice-Hall.

Bartolla, C.; Miller, S.J.; and Dinitz, S. 1976. *Juvenile Victimization: The Institutional Paradox*. New York: Halsted Press.

Barton, A. 1955. "On the Concept of Property Space in Social Research." In *The Language of Social Research*, ed. P.F. Lazarsfeld and M. Rosenberg. Glencoe, Ill.: Free Press.

Beasley, R.W., and Antunes, G. 1974. "The Etiology of Urban Crime: An Ecological Analysis." *Criminology* 4:439-461.

Biderman, A.D., and Reiss, A.J. 1967. "On Exploring the 'Dark Figure' of Crime." *Annals of the American Academy of Political and Social Sciences* 374 (November):1-15.

Binder, A., and Scharf, P. 1980. "The Violent Police-Citizen Encounter." In *The Police and Violence*, ed. L.J. Sherman. *The Annals* 452 (November).

Black, D.J. 1970. "Production of Crime Rates." *American Sociological Review* 35 (August):733-748.

Black, S. 1963. "A Reporter at Large—Burglary I." *New Yorker* (December 7):63-128.

Block, R. 1979. "Community Environment and Violent Crime." *Criminology* 17 (1):46-57.

Boggs, S.L. 1965. "Urban Crime Patterns." *American Sociological Review* 30 (December):899-908.

Bohmer, C. 1974. "Judicial Attitudes Toward Rape Victims." *Judicature* 57 (February).

Boland, B. 1976. "Patterns of Urban Crime." In *Sample Surveys of the Victims of Crime*, ed. W.G. Skogan. Cambridge, Mass.: Ballinger.

Bonger, W.A. 1961. *Criminality and Economic Conditions*. Boston: Little, Brown.

Booth, A.; Johnson, D.R.; and Choldin, H.M. 1977. "Correlates of City Crime Rates: Victimization Surveys versus Official Statistics." *Social Problems* 25:187-197.

Booth, A.; Welch, S.; and Johnson, D.R. 1976. "Crowding and Urban Crime Rates." *Urban Affairs Quarterly* 11:291-307.

Bordua, D.J. 1958-1959. "Juvenile Delinquency and 'Anomie': An Attempt at Replication." *Social Problems* 6 (Winter):230-238.

Bowker, L.H. 1980. *Prison Victimization*. New York: Elsevier.

Burgess, A.W., and Holmstrom, L.L. 1975. "Rape: The Victim and the Criminal Justice System." In *Crimes, Victims, and Justice*. Victimology: A New Focus, ed. I. Drapkin and E. Viano, vol. III. Lexington, Mass.: Lexington Books, D.C. Heath.

Butler, R.N. 1975. *Why Survive?* New York: Harper and Row.

Butler, R.N., and Lewis, M.I. 1977. *Aging and Mental Health*. St. Louis: Mosby.

Calhoun, J.B. 1963. "Population Density and Social Pathology." In *The Urban Condition*, ed. L. Duhl. New York: Basic Books.

Campbell, T., and Fiske, D.W. 1959. "Convergent and Discriminant Validation by Multitrait-Multimethod Matrix." *Psychological Bulletin*, 56 (March):81-105.

Caplovitz, D. 1963. *The Poor Pay More*. New York: Free Press.

Carnahan, D.; Guest, A.M.; and Galle, O.R. 1974. "Congestion, Concentration and Behavior: Research in the Study of Urban Population Density." *The Sociological Quarterly* 15 (Autumn):488-506.

Chapman, S.G. 1971. "Police Patrol Administration." In *Municipal Police Administration*, ed. G.D. Eastman and E.M. Eastman, pp. 77-128. Washington, D.C. International City Management Association.

Chase, N.F. 1975. *A Child Is Being Beaten*. New York: McGraw-Hill.

Chilton, R.J. 1964. "Continuity in Delinquency Area Research: A

Comparison of Studies for Baltimore, Detroit, and Indianapolis.'' *American Sociological Review* 29 (February):71-83.

Clemente, F., and Kleinman, M.B. 1976. "Fear of Crime among the Aged.'' *Gerontologist* 16 (3):207-210

Clinard, M.B. 1968. *Sociology of Deviant Behavior.* New York: Holt, Rinehart and Winston.

Cohen, A.K. 1955. *Delinquent Boys: The Culture of the Group.* Glencoe: The Free Press.

Cohen, J., and Cohen, P. 1975. *Applied Multiple Regression/Correlation Analysis for the Behavioral Sciences.* Hillsdale, N.J.: Lawrence Erlbaum Associates.

Cohen, L.E., and Felson, M. 1979. "Social Change and Crime Rate Trends.'' *American Sociological Review* 44 (August):588-608.

Cohen, L.E.; Felson, M.; and Land, K.C. 1980. "A Macrodynamic Analysis, 1947-1977, with Ex Ante Forecasts for the Mid-1980s.'' *American Journal of Sociology* 86 (July):90-118.

Cook, F.L. 1976. "Criminal Victimization of the Elderly: A New National Problem? In *Victims and Society*, ed. E.C. Viano. Washington, D.C.: Visage Press.

Cook, F.L., and Cook, T.D. 1976. "Evaluating the Rhetoric of Crisis: A Case Study of Criminal Victimization of the Elderly.'' *Social Service Review* 50:632-646.

Cunningham, C.L. 1976. "Pattern and Effect of Crime against the Aging: The Kansas City Study.'' In *Crime and the Elderly*, ed. J. Goldsmith and S.S. Goldsmith. Lexington, Mass.: Lexington Books, D.C. Heath.

Curtis, L.A. 1975. *Violence, Race, and Culture.* Lexington, Mass.: Lexington Books, D.C. Heath.

Dadrian, V.N. 1976. "An Attempt at Defining Victimology.'' In *Victims and Society*, ed. E.C. Viano. Washington, D.C.: Visage Press.

Decker, D.L. 1980. *Social Gerontology.* Boston: Little, Brown.

Decker, D.L.; O'Brien, R.M.; and Shichor, D., 1979. "Patterns of Juvenile Victimization and Urban Structure.'' In *Perspectives on Victimology*, ed. W.H. Parsonage, pp. 88-98. Beverly Hills: Sage Publications.

Decker, S.H. 1977. "Official Crime Rates and Victim Surveys: An Empirical Comparison.'' *Journal of Criminal Justice* 5:47-54.

———. 1978. "Crime and Victimization: A Structural Approach.'' Paper presented at the Annual Meeting of the American Society of Criminology, Dallas, November.

DeFleur, L.B. 1967. "Ecological Variables in the Cross-Cultural Study of Delinquency.'' *Social Forces* 45 (June):556-570.

Denno, D., and Cramer, J.A. 1976. "The Effects of Victim Characteristics on Judicial Decision Making.'' In *Criminal Justice and the Victim*, ed. W.F. McDonald. Beverly Hills, Calif.: Sage.

Diamond, A.S. 1935. *Primitive Law*. London: Longmans.

Doerner, W.G. 1978. "The Index of Southerness Revisited: The Influence of Where From upon Whodunnit." *Criminology* 16 (May):47-59.

Dror, Y. 1971. *Public Policymaking Reexamined*. Scranton: Chandler.

Duncan, O.D. 1964. "Social Organization and the Ecosystem." In *Handbook of Modern Sociology*, ed. R.E.L. Faris. Chicago: Rand McNally.

Dynes, R.R., and Quarantelli, E.L. 1974. "Organizations as Victims in Mass Civil Disturbances." In *Victimology*, ed. I. Drapkin and E. Viano. Lexington, Mass.: Lexington Books, D.C. Heath.

Edelherz, H. and Geis, G. 1974. *Public Compensation to Victims of Crime*. New York: Praeger.

Edwards, C. 1971. *The Hammurabi Code*. Port Washington, N.Y.: Kennikat Press.

Ellenberger, H. 1954. "Relations Psychologiques Entre le Criminel et la Victime." *Revue Internationale de Criminologie et de Police Technique* 3 (2). (Quoted in Reckless 1973.)

Elmer, M.C. 1933. "Century-Old Ecological Studies in France." *American Journal of Sociology* 39 (July):63-70.

Empey, L.T. 1978. *American Delinquency: Its Meaning and Construction*. Homewood, Ill.: Dorsey Press.

Ennis, P.H. 1967. *Criminal Victimization in the United States: A Report of National Surveys*. The President's Commission on Law Enforcement and Administration of Justice. Washington, D.C.: U.S. Government Printing Office.

Faris, R.E.L. 1967. *Chicago Sociology, 1920-1932*. Chicago: University of Chicago Press.

Faris, R.E.L., and Dunham, H.W. 1939. *Mental Disorders in Urban Areas: An Ecological Study of Schizophrenia and Other Psychoses*. Chicago: University of Chicago Press.

Fattah, E.A. 1967. "Vers une Typologie Criminologique des Victimes." *Revue Internationale de Police Criminelle* 209 (July-August):162-169.

Federal Bureau of Investigation. 1974. *Uniform Crime Report 1973*. Washington, D.C.: U.S. Government Printing Office.

_____. 1975. *Uniform Crime Report 1974*. Washington, D.C.: U.S. Government Printing Office.

Feyerherm, W.H., and Hindelang, M.J. 1974. "On the Victimization of Juveniles: Some Preliminary Results." *Journal of Research in Crime and Delinquency* 11 (January):40-50.

Finestone, H. 1976. "The Delinquent and Society: The Shaw and McKay Tradition." In *Delinquency, Crime and Society*, ed. J.R. Short, Jr. Chicago: University of Chicago Press.

Fletcher, J. 1848. "Moral and Educational Statistics of England and Wales." *Journal of the Statistical Society of London* 2: 344-366.

Fooner, M. 1967. "Adventitious Criminality: A Crime Pattern in an Affluent Society." *International Criminal Police Review* 22: 246-250.

Freedman, J. 1973. "The Effects of Population Density on Humans." In *Psychological Perspectives on Population*, ed. J. Fawcet. New York: Basic Books.

Freedman, J.; Heshka, S.; and Levy, A. 1975. "Population Density and Pathology: Is There a Relationship?" *Journal of Experimental Social Psychology* 11 (November):539-552.

Friedman, C.J.; Mann, F.; and Adelman, H. 1976. "Juvenile Street Gangs The Victimization of Youth." *Adolescence* 11 (Winter).

Fry, M. 1957. "Justice for Victims." *The Observer* (London), July 7.

Furstenberg, F.F. 1971. "Public Reaction to Crime in the Streets." *American Scholar* 40 (Autumn):601-622.

Galaway, B., and Hudson, J. 1975. "Restitution and Rehabilitation: Some Central Issues." In *Considering the Victim: Readings in Restitution and Victim Compensation*, ed. J. Hudson and B. Galaway. Springfield, Ill.: Charles C Thomas.

Galaway, B., and Hudson, J. eds. 1981. *Perspectives on Crime Victims*. St. Louis: C.V. Mosby.

Galle, O.; Gove, W.R., and McPherson, J.M. 1972. "Population Density and Pathology: What Are the Relationships for Man?" *Science* 176 (April):23-30.

Galle, O.; McCarthy, J.D.; and Gove, W.R. 1974. "Population Density and Pathology." Paper presented at the Annual Meeting of the Population Association of America, New York.

Garabedian, P.G. 1964. "Social Roles in a Correctional Community." *Journal of Criminal Law, Criminology, and Police Science* 55 (September):338-347.

Gastil, R.D. 1971. "Homicide and a Regional Culture of Violence." *American Sociological Review* 36 (June):412-427.

Geis, G. 1977. "Restitution by Criminal Offenders: A Summary and Overview." In *Restitution in Criminal Justice*, ed. J. Hudson and B. Galaway. Lexington, Mass.: Lexington Books, D.C. Heath.

Georges, D.E., and Harries, K.D. Forthcoming. *Crime: A Spatial Perspective*. New York: Columbia University Press.

Gibbons, D.C. 1975. "Offender Typologies—Two Decades Later." *British Journal of Criminology* 15 (April):140-156.

————. 1977. *Society, Crime, and Criminal Careers*. Englewood Cliffs, N.J.: Prentice-Hall.

Gil, D.G. 1970. *Violence Against Children*. Cambridge, Mass.: Harvard University Press.

Glaser, B.G., and Strauss, A.L. 1967. *The Discovery of Grounded Theory: Strategies for Qualitative Research*. Chicago: Aldine.

Glaser, D. 1972. *Adult Crime and Social Policy*. Englewood Cliffs, N.J.: Prentice-Hall.

Glyde, J. 1856. "Localities of Crime in Suffolk." *Journal of the Statistical Society of London* 19: 102-106.

Goldsmith, J., and Goldsmith, S.S. eds. 1976. *Crime and the Elderly: Challenge and Response*. Lexington, Mass.: Lexington Books, D.C. Heath.

Gordon, R.A. 1967. "Issues in the Ecological Study of Delinquency." *American Sociological Review* 32 (December):927-944.

_____. 1968. "Issues in Multiple Regression." *American Journal of Sociology* 73 (March):592-616.

Gove, W.R., and Hughes, M. 1980. "Reexaminig the Ecological Fallacy: A Study in Which Aggregate Data are Critical in Investigating the Pathological Effects of Living Alone." *Social Forces* 58 (June):1157-1177.

Gove, W.R.; Hughes, M.; and Galle, O. 1979. "Overcrowding in the Home." *American Sociological Review* 44 (February):59-80.

Greenwood, M.J., and Wadycki, W.J. 1973. "Crime Rates and Public Expenditures for Police Protection: Their Interaction." *Review of Social Economy* 31 (October):138-151.

Gubrium, J.F. 1974. "Victimization in Old Age." *Crime and Deliquency* 20 (July):245-250.

Guerry, A.M. 1833. "Essai sur la Statistique Morale de la France." (Quoted in *Westminster Review*, vol. 18.)

Hackney, S. 1969. "Southern Violence." In *The History of Violence in America*, ed. H.D. Graham and T.R. Gurt, pp. 505-527. New York: Bantam.

Hage, J. 1972. *Techniques and Problems of Theory Construction in Sociology*. New York: Wiley.

Harland, A.T. 1981. "Victim Compensation Programs and Issues." In *Perspective on Crime Victims*, ed. B. Galaway and J. Hudson. St. Louis: C.V. Mosby.

Harries, K.D. 1971. "The Geography of American Crime, 1968." *Journal of Geography* 70: 204-213.

_____. 1973. "Social Indicators and Metropolitan Variations in Crime." *Proceedings, Association of American Geographers* 5: 97-101.

_____. 1974. *The Geography of Crime and Justice*. New York: McGraw-Hill.

_____. 1976. "Cities and Crime: A Geographic Model." *Criminology* 14 (November):369-386.

_____. 1980. *Crime and Environment*. Springfield, Ill.: Charles C. Thomas.

Harries, K.D., and Brunn, S.D. 1978. *The Geography of Laws and Justice*. New York: Praeger.

Hawley, A.H. 1981. *Urban Society: An Ecological Approach*. New York: Ronald Press.

Hemley, D.D., and McPheters, L.R. 1974. "Crime as an Externality of Regional Economic Growth." *Review of Regional Studies* 4 (3):73-84.

Hendricks, J., and Hendricks, C.D. 1977. *Aging in Mass Society: Myths and Realities*. Cambridge, Mass.: Winthrop.

Hepburn, R., and Monti, D.J. 1979. "Victimization, Fear of Crime, and Adaptive Responses among High School Students." In *Perspectives on Victimology*, ed. W.H. Parsonage, pp. 121-132. Beverly Hills, Calif.: Sage.

Herbert, D. 1977. "Crime, Delinquency and the Urban Environment." *Progress in Human Geography* 1:208-239.

Hindelang, M.J. 1976. *Criminal Victimization in Eight American Cities*. Cambridge, Mass.: Ballinger.

_____. 1978. "Race and Involvement in Crimes." *American Sociological Review* 43 (1):93-109.

Holmstrom, L.L., and Burgess, A.W. 1975. "Rape: The Victim Goes on Trial." In *Crimes, Victims, and Justice*. Victimology: A New Focus, ed. I. Drapkin and E. Viano, vol. III. Lexington, Mass.: Lexington Books, D.C. Heath.

Hood, R., and Sparks, R. 1970. *Key Issues in Criminology*. London: Weidenfeld and Nicolson.

Jacobs, J. 1961. *The Death and Life of Great American Cities*. New York: Random House.

Jeffrey, C.R. 1971. *Crime Prevention through Environmental Design*. Beverly Hills, Calif.: Sage.

Joly, H. 1889. *La France Criminelle*. Paris: Cerf.

Jonassen, C.T. 1949. "A Re-evaluation and Critique of the Logic and Some Methods of Shaw and McKay." *American Sociological Review* 14 (October):608-614.

Kirmeyer, S.L. 1978. "Urban Density and Pathology: A Review of Research." *Environment and Behavior* 10 (June):247-269.

Knudten, M.S., and Knudten, R.D. 1981. "What Happens to Crime Victims and Witnesses in the Justice System?" In *Perspectives on Crime Victims*, ed. B. Galaway and J. Hudson. St. Louis: C.V. Mosby.

Kvalseth, T.O. 1975. "Statistical Models of Urban Crime: A Study of Burglary." Paper presented at the Joint National Meeting of the Operations Research Society of America and the Institute of Management Sciences, Las Vegas, November 17-19.

_____. 1977. "A Note on the Effects of Population Density and Unemployment on Urban Crime." *Criminology* 15 (1):105-110.

Labowitz, B.D. 1975. "Age and Fearfulness: Personal and Situational Factors." *Journal of Gerontology* 30:696-700.

Lalli, M. and Savitz, L.D. 1976. "The Fear of Crime in the School Enterprise and Its Consequences." *Education and Urban Society* 8 (August): 401-416.

Lamborn, L.L. 1980. "The Impact of Victimology on the Criminal Law." Paper presented at the Annual Meeting of the American Society of Criminology, San Francisco, November.

_____. 1981. "Victim Compensation Programs: An Overview." In *Perspectives on Crime Victims*, ed. B. Galaway and J. Hudson. St. Louis: C.V. Mosby.

Lander, B. 1954. *Understanding of Juvenile Delinquency*. New York: Columbia University Press.

Laster, R.E. 1975. "Criminal Restitution: A Survey of its Past History." *Considering the Victim*, ed. J. Hudson and B. Galaway. Springfield, Ill.: Charles C Thomas.

Lazarsfeld, P.F. 1972. "Some Remarks on Typological Procedures in Social Research." In *Continuities in the Language of Social Research*, ed. P.F. Lazarsfeld, A.K. Pasanella, and M. Rosenberg. New York: Macmillan.

Levin, Y., and Lindesmith, A. 1937. "English Ecology and Criminology of the Past Century." *Journal of Criminal Law, Criminology and Police Science* 27(6):801-816.

Levine, J.P. 1976. "The Potential for Crime Overreporting in Criminal Victimization Surveys." *Criminology* 14 (December):307-330.

Lindsey, D.B. 1980. "Police as Victim." Paper presented at the Annual Meeting of the American Society of Criminology, San Francisco, November.

Littrell, W.B. 1976. "Editor's Introduction." In *Current Issues in Social Policy*, ed. W.B. Littrell and G. Sjoberg. Beverly Hills, Calif.: Sage.

Loftin, C., and Hill, R.H. 1974. "Regional Subculture and Homicide: An Examination of the Gastil-Hackney Thesis." *American Sociological Review* 39 (October):714-724.

Lorenz, K. 1967. *On Aggression*. London: Methuen.

McCarthy, J.D.; Galle, O.R.; and Zimmern, W. 1975. "Population Density, Social Structure, and Interpersonal Violence: An Intermetropolitan Test of Competing Models." *American Behavioral Scientist* 18 (July-August):771-791.

McDonald, W.F., ed. 1976. *Criminal Justice and the Victim*. Beverly Hills, Calif.: Sage.

McKinney, J.C. 1966. *Constructive Typology and Social Theory*. New York: Appleton-Century-Crofts.

Maine, H.S. 1887. *Ancient Law*. London: John Murray.

Maltz, M.D. 1977. "Crime Statistics: A Historical Perspective." *Crime and Delinquency* 23:32-40.

Mayhew, B.H., and Levinger, R.L. 1976. "Size and the Density of Interaction in Human Aggregates." *American Journal of Sociology* 82 (April): 86-110.

Mayhew, H., and Binny, J.J. 1862. *The Criminal Prisons of London*. London:Charles Griffin.

Meiners, R.E. 1978. *Victim Compensation: Economic, Legal, and Political Aspects.* Lexington, Mass.: Lexington Books, D.C. Heath.

Mendelsohn, B. 1956. "Victimology." *Etudes Internationales de Psycho-Sociologie Criminelle* (July-September):23-26.

_____. 1963. "The Origin of the Doctrine of Victimology." *Excerpta Criminologica* 3:239-244.

_____ . 1975. "Victimology and the Technical and Social Sciences: A Call for the Establishment of Victimological Clinics." In *Theoretical Issues in Victimology.* Victimology: A New Focus, ed. I. Drapkin and E. Viano, vol. I. Lexington, Mass.: Lexington Books, D.C. Heath.

Merton, R.K. 1938. "Social Structure and Anomie." *American Sociological Review* 3 (October):672-682.

Milakovich, M.E., and Weis, K. 1975. "Politics and Measures of Success in the War on Crime." *Crime and Delinquency* 21:1-10.

Miller, W.B. 1958. "Lower Class Culture as a Generating Milieu of Gang Delinquency." *The Journal of Social Issues* 14:315-319.

Mladenka, K.R., and Hill, K.Q. 1976. "A Reexamination of the Etiology of Urban Crime." *Criminology* 13 (4):491-506.

Morris, T. 1957. *The Criminal Area.* London: Routledge and Kegan Paul.

_____ . 1971. "Some Ecological Studies of the 19th Century." *Ecology, Crime and Delinquency,* ed. H.L. Voss and D.M. Petersen. New York: Appleton-Century-Crofts.

Nelson, J.F. 1978. "Alternative Measures of Crime: A Comparison of the Uniform Crime Report and the National Crime Survey in 26 American Cities." Paper presented at the Annual Meeting of the American Society of Criminology, Dallas.

Nettler, G. 1978. *Explaining Crime,* 2nd ed. New York: McGraw-Hill.

Newman, D.J. 1966. *Conviction: The Determination of Guilt or Innocence without Trial.* Boston: Little, Brown.

Newman, O. 1972. *Defensible Space: Design for the Improvement of Security in Urban Residential Areas.* New York: Macmillan.

Nie, H.; Hull, C.H.; Jenkins, J.G.; Steinbrenner, K.; and Bent, D.H. 1975. *Statistical Package for the Social Sciences.* New York: McGraw-Hill.

Normandeau, A. 1968. "Patterns in Robbery." *Criminologica* 6 (November):2-15.

O'Brien, R.M.; Shichor, D.; and Decker, D.L. 1978. "Urban Structure and Household Victimization of the Elderly." Paper presented at the Ninth World Congress of Sociology, Uppsala, August.

O'Brien, R.M.; Shichor, D.; and Decker, D.L. 1980. "An Empirical Comparison of the Validity of UCR and NCS Crime Rates." *Sociological Quarterly* 21 (Summer):391-401.

Pecar, J. 1972. "Involved Bystanders: Examination of a Neglected Aspect of Criminology and Victimology." *International Journal of Contemporary Sociology* (July-October):81-87.

Penick, B.K.E., and Owens, M.E.B., III, eds. 1976. *Surveying Crime.* Washington, D.C.: National Academy of Sciences.

Piazza, T. 1980. "The Analysis of Attitude Items." *American Journal of Sociology* 86 (November):584-603.

Pike, L.O. 1873. *A History of Crime in England.* London: Smith, Elder.

Piliavin, I., and Briar, S. 1964. "Police Encounters with Juveniles." *American Journal of Sociology* 70:206-214.

Pokorny, A. 1965. "Human Violence: A Comparison of Homicide, Aggravated Assault, Suicide and Attempted Suicide." *Journal of Criminal Law, Criminology, and Police Science* 56:488-497.

Pope, C.E. 1979. "Victimization Rates and Neighborhood Characteristics: Some Preliminary Findings." In *Perspectives on Victimology,* ed. W.H. Parsonage. Beverly Hills, Calif.: Sage.

President's Commission on Law Enforcement and Administration of Justice. 1967. *The Challenge of Crime in a Free Society.* Washington, D.C.: U.S. Government Printing Office.

Pressman, I., and Carol, A. 1971. "Crime as a Diseconomy of Scale." *Review of Social Economy* 29 (October):227-236.

Pritchard, J.B. 1955. *Ancient Near Eastern Texts Relating to the Old Testament.* Princeton: Princeton University Press.

Quetelet, L.A.J. 1842. *A Treatise on Man.* Edinburgh: Chambers.

Quinney, R. 1966. "Structural Characteristics, Population Areas, and Crime Rates in the United States." *Journal of Criminal Law, Criminology, and Police Science* 57 1:45-52.

Rapoport, A. 1975. "Toward a Redefinition of Density." *Environment and Behavior* 7 (June):133-158.

Rawson, R.W. 1839. "An Inquiry into the Statistics of Crime in England and Wales." *Journal of the Statistical Society of London* 2:316-344.

Reckless, W.C. 1973. *The Crime Problem.* Englewood Cliffs, N.J.: Prentice-Hall.

Reiff, R. 1979. *The Invisible Victim.* New York: Basic Books.

Reissman, L. 1964. *The Urban Process.* New York: Free Press.

Reppetto, T.A. 1974. *Residential Crime.* Cambridge, Mass.: Ballinger.

Robinson, W.S. 1950. "Ecological Correlations and Behavior of Individuals." *American Sociological Review* 15 (June):351-358.

Rodman, H. 1968. "Family and Social Pathology in the Ghetto." *Science* 161 (August):756-762.

Roebuck, J.B. 1967. *Criminal Typology.* Springfield, Ill.: Charles C Thomas.

Roncek, D.W. 1975. "Density and Crime: A Methodological Critique." *American Behavioral Scientist* 18 (July-August):843-860.

Rosen, L., and Turner, S.H. 1967. "An Evaluation of the Lander Approach to Ecology of Delinquency." *Social Problems* 15 (Fall):189-200.

Rosenblum, R.H., and Blew, C.H. 1979. *Victim/Witness Assistance.* Washington, D.C.: U.S. Government Printing Office.

Rubenstein, J. 1973. *City Police*. New York: Farrar, Straus and Giroux.

Schafer, S. 1977. *Victimology: The Victim and His Criminal*. Reston, Va.: Reston.

Schmidt, C.F. 1960*a*. "Urban Crime Areas: Part I." *American Sociological Review* 25 (August):527-542.

————. 1960*b*. "Urban Crime Areas: Part II." *American Sociological Review* 25 (October):655-678.

Schmidt, D.E.; Goldman, R.P.; and Flimer, N.R. 1979. "Perceptions of Crowding: Predicting at the Residence, Neighborhood, and City Levels," *Environment and Behavior* 11 (March):105-130.

Schneider, A.L., and Schneider, P.S. 1981. "Victim Assistance Programs: An Overview." In *Perspectives on Crime Victims*, ed. B. Galaway and J. Hudson. St. Louis: C.V. Mosby.

Schrag, C. "A Preliminary Criminal Typology." *Pacific Sociological Review* (Spring):11-16.

————. 1967. "Elements of Theoretical Analysis in Sociology." In *Sociological Theory: Inquiries and Paradigms*, ed. L. Gross. New York: Harper and Row.

Schuessler, K. 1962. "Components of Variation in City Crime Rates." *Social Problems* 9 (Spring):314-323.

Schur, E.M. 1969. *Our Criminal Society: The Social and Legal Sources of Crime*. Englewood Cliffs, N.J.: Prentice-Hall.

Seidman, D., and Couzens, M. 1974. "Getting the Crime Rate Down: Political Pressure and Crime Reporting." *Law and Society Review* 8: 457-493.

Sellin, T., and Wolfgang, M.E. 1964. *The Measurement of Delinquency*. New York: Wiley.

Selltiz, C.; Wrightsman, L.S.; and Cook, S. 1976. *Research Methods in Social Relations*. New York: Holt, Rinehart, and Winston.

Sengstock, M.C., and Liang, J. 1979. "Elderly Victims of Crime: A Refinement of Theory in Victimology." Paper presented at the Third International Symposium of Victimology, Münster, September.

Shaw, C.R., and McKay, H.D. 1929. *Delinquency Areas*. Chicago: University of Chicago Press.

Shaw, C.R., and McKay, H.D. 1931. *Social Factors in Juvenile Delinquency*. Washington, D.C.: U.S. Government Printing Office.

Shaw, C.R., and McKay, H.D. 1969. *Juvenile Delinquency and Urban Areas*, rev. ed. Chicago: University of Chicago Press.

Sheleff, L.S. 1974. "The Criminal Triad—Bystander, Victim, Criminal." *International Journal of Criminology and Penology* 2: 159-172.

Sheleff, L.S., and Shichor, D. 1980. "Victimological Aspects of Bystander Involvement." *Crime and Delinquency* 26 (April): 193-201.

Shichor, D. 1975. "The Wrongfully Accused and the Criminal Justice System." In *Crimes, Victims, and Justice*. Victimology: A New Focus, ed. I. Drapkin and E. Viano, vol. III. Lexington, Mass.: Lexington Books, D.C. Heath.

Shichor, D.; Decker, D.L.; and O'Brien, R.M. 1979. "Population Density and Criminal Victimization: Some Unexpected Findings in Central Cities." *Criminology* 17 (August):184-193.

―――. 1980. "The Relationship of Criminal Victimization, Police per Capita and Population Density in Twenty-six Cities." *Journal of Criminal Justice* 8:309-316.

Shover, N. 1973. "The Social Organization of Burglary." *Social Problems* 20:499-514.

Skogan, W.G. "The Validity of Official Crime Statistics: An Empirical Investigation." *Social Science Quarterly* 55:25-38.

―――. 1976. "Crime and Crime Rates." In *Sample Survey of the Victims of Crime*, ed. W.G. Skogan. Cambridge, Mass.: Ballinger.

―――. 1977a. "The Changing Distribution of Big-City Crime: A Multi-City Time-Series Analysis." *Urban Affairs Quarterly* 13 (1):33-48.

―――. 1977b. "Dimension of the Dark Figure of Unreported Crime." *Crime and Delinquency* 23 (January):41-50.

Slatin, G.I. 1969. "Ecological Analysis of Delinquency Aggregation Effects." *American Sociological Review* 34 (December):894-907.

Smigel, E.O., and Ross, H.L. 1970. *Crimes Against Bureaucracy*. New York: Van Nostrand Reinhold.

Spector, P.E. 1975. "Population Density and Unemployment: The Effects on the Incidence of Violent Crime in the American City." *Criminology* 12 (February):399-401.

Sundeen, R.A., and Mathieu, J.T. 1976. "The Urban Elderly: Environments of Fear." In *Crime and the Elderly*, ed. J. Goldsmith and S.S. Goldsmith. Lexington, Mass.: Lexington Books, D.C. Heath.

Sutherland, E.H. 1937. *The Professional Thief*. Chicago: University of Chicago Press.

Sutherland, E.H., and Cressey, D.R. 1960. *Principles of Criminology*, 6th ed. Philadelphia: Lippincott.

Sutherland, E.H., and Cressey, D.R. 1978. *Criminology*, 10th ed. Philadelphia: Lippincott.

Swimmer, G. 1974. "Relationship of Police and Crime: Some Methodological and Empirical Results." *Criminology* 12 (November):293-314.

Sykes, G.M. 1958. *The Society of Captives*. Princeton: Princeton University Press.

Tittle, C.R.; Willemer, W.J.; and Smith, D.A. 1978. "The Myth of Social Class and Criminality." *American Sociological Review* 43:643-656.

U.S. Bureau of the Census. 1976. *Statistical Abstract of the United States: 1976*, 97th ed. Washington, D.C.

―――. 1973. *County and City Data Book, 1972*. Washington, D.C.: U.S. Government Printing Office.

U.S. Department of Health, Education and Welfare. 1977. *Violent Schools—*

Safe Schools: The Safe School Study Report to the Congress. Washington, D.C.: U.S. Government Printing Office.

U.S. Department of Justice. 1974. *Expenditures and Employment Data for the Criminal Justice System, 1974*. Washington, D.C.: U.S. Government Printing Office.

_____ . 1975. *Criminal Victimization Surveys in 13 American Cities*. Washington, D.C.: U.S. Government Printing Office.

_____ . 1976*a*. *Criminal Victimization Surveys in Eight American Cities*. Washington, D.C.: U.S. Government Printing Office.

_____ . 1976*b*. *Criminal Victimization Surveys in Chicago, Detroit, Los Angeles, New York, Philadephia*. Washington, D.C.: U.S. Government Printing Office.

_____ . 1976*c*. *Criminal Victimization in the United States*. Washington, D.C.: U.S. Government Printing Office.

_____ . 1977. *Criminal Victimization in the United States: Comparison of 1975 and 1976 Findings*. Washington, D.C.: U.S. Government Printing Office.

U.S. House of Representatives. 1977. *In Search of Security: A National Perspective on Elderly Crime Victimization*. Washington, D.C.: U.S. Government Printing Office.

van den Berghe, P.L. 1974. "Bringing Beasts Back In: Toward a Biosocial Theory of Aggression." *American Sociological Review* 39 (6):777-788.

Von Hentig, H. 1948. *The Criminal and His Victim*. New Haven: Yale University Press.

Voss, H.L., and Petersen, D.M., eds. 1971. *Ecology, Crime and Delinquency*. New York: Appleton-Century-Crofts.

Walker, N. 1971. *Crimes, Courts and Figures: An Introduction to Criminal Statistics*. Middlesex: Penguin Books.

Weathersby, G.B. 1970. "Some Determinants of Crime: An Econometric Analysis of Major and Minor Crimes Around Boston." Paper presented at the Thirty-Eighth National Meeting of the Operations Research Society of America, Ann Arbor, October.

White, R.C. 1932. "A Study of Residence and Place of Offense of Felons in Indianapolis." *Social Forces* 10:498-509.

Wilks, J.A. 1967. "Ecological Correlates of Crime and Delinquency." In *Task Force Report: Crime and Its Impact—An Assessment*. Washington, D.C.: U.S. Government Printing Office.

Williams, K.M. 1976. "The Effects of Victim Characteristics on the Disposition of Violent Crimes." In *Criminal Justice and the Victim*, ed. W.F. McDonald. Beverly Hills, Calif.: Sage.

Wilson, J.Q. 1968. *Varieties of Police Behavior*. Cambridge, Mass.: Harvard University Press.

_____ . 1970. "Crime." In *Toward a National Urban Policy*, ed. D.P. Moynihan. New York: Basic Books.

Wilson, J.Q., and Boland, B. 1976. "Crime." In *The Urban Predicament*, ed. G. Williams and N. Glazer. Washington, D.C.: Urban Institute.

Winch, R.F. 1947. "Heruistic and Empirical Typologies." *American Sociological Review* 12 (February):68-75.

Wirth, L. 1938. "Urbanism as a Way of Life." *American Journal of Sociology* 44:1-24.

Wolfgang, M.E. 1958. *Patterns in Criminal Homicide*. Philadelphia: University of Pennsylvania Press.

――――. 1968. "Urban Crime." In *The Metropolitan Enigma*, ed. J.Q. Wilson. Cambridge, Mass.: Harvard University Press.

――――. 1979. "Basic Concepts in Victimological Theory." Keynote lecture, Third International Symposium on Victimology, Münster, September.

Wolfgang, M.E., and Ferracuti, F. 1962. "Subculture of Violence: An Interpretive Analysis of Homicide." *International Annals of Criminology* 1:1-9

Wolfgang, M.E., and Ferracuti, F. 1967. *Subculture of Violence*. London: Social Science Paperbacks.

Wolfgang, M.E.; Figlio, R.M.; and Sellin, T. 1972. *Delinquency in a Birth Cohort*. Chicago: University of Chicago Press.

Wolfgang, M.E.; Savitz, L.; and Johnston, N. 1970. *Sociology of Crime and Delinquency*. New York: Wiley.

Wolfgang, M.E., and Singer, S.I. 1978. "Victim Categories of Crime." *Journal of Criminal Law and Criminology* 69 (Novemer):379-394.

Wood, A.L. 1969. "Ideal and Empirical Typologies for Research in Deviance and Control." *Sociology and Social Research* 53 (January):227-241.

Young Rifai, M.A. 1976. *Older Americans' Research Project: Final Report*. Portland: Multnomah County Division of Public Safety Community Affairs/Crime Prevention Unit.

――――. 1977. *Justice and Older Americans*. Lexington, Mass.: Lexington Books, D.C. Heath.

Ziegenhagen, E.A. 1977. *Victims, Crime and Social Control*. New York: Praeger.

Index

Age-specific crime, 65
Aggregate-level data, 18
Alker, H.R., Jr., 18, 49
Althauser, R.P., 26
Althauser, R.P., and Heberlein, T.A., 26
Amir, M., 5, 71
Angel, S., 56, 78
Anglo-Saxon law, 3
Antunes, G.E., et al., 74
Areal density, 46
Assault, simple/aggravated, 32, 33, 34, 38-42, 48, 49, 50, 51, 79; definitions, 85, 86; and juvenile victimization, 68, 69. *See also* Nonproperty assaultive crimes
Atlanta, 19, 35, 46

Bakan, D., 65
Baldassare, M., 46, 47
Balkin, S., 37, 41
Baltimore, 15, 19, 35, n.4
Barnes, H.E., and Teeters, N.K., 6
Bartolla, C., Miller, S.J., and Dinitz, S., 10
Barton, A., 37
Beasley, R.W., and Antunes, G., 15-16, 28, 45, 59
Belgium, 13
Biderman, A.D., and Reiss, A.J., 22, 35
Binder, A., and Scharf, P., 10
Biologically weak victims, 6
Black, D.J., 22
Blacks: and juvenile victimization, 71
Block, R., 16
Blood feuds, 2-3
Blue-collar population, percentage of: and elderly victimization, 77, 78; and juvenile victimization, 69
Boggs, S.L., 16, 28, 56, 57, 60
Boland, 17, 28, 46, 57, 72, 77
Bonger, W.A., 37

Booth, A., Johnson, D.R., and Choldin, H.M., 18, 24, 34, 55
Booth, A., Welch, S., and Johnson, D.R., 48, 60
Bordua, D.J., 15
Boston, 19
Buffalo, 19
Burglary, 30, 32, 33, 34, 38, 49, 50, 52, 79; definitions, 85, 86; and elderly victimization, 74, 75, 76, 78; household, 60, 61; and juvenile victimization, 67, 71
Butler, R.N., 73
Butler, R.N., and Lewis, M.I., 73
Bystanders, 10

Calhoun, J.B., 56, 60
Campbell, T., and Fiske, D.W., 26
Caplovitz, D., 9
Carnahan, D., Guest, A.M., and Galle, O.R., 46-47
Chapman, S.G., 56
Chase, N.F., 65
Chicago, 14-15, 16, 19
Chilton, R.J., 15
Cincinnati, 19
Civil disturbances, 9
Civil law (torts), 3, 4
Clemente, F., and Kleinman, M.B., 73, 74
Cleveland, 19, 35 n.4
Clinard, M.B., 18
Clinard, M.B., and Quinney, R., 37
Cohen, A.K., 28
Cohen, J., and Cohen, P., 61, 72, 76
Cohen, L.E., and Felson, M., 52
Cohen, L.E., Felson, M., and Land, K.C., 53
Collective responsibility, 2-3
Commercial crimes, defined, 86
Commercial establishments, 83-84
Compensation programs, 7-8, 11
Convergent validation, 26-27, 30, 32-33, 34

Cook, F.L., 10
Cook, F.L., and Cook, T.D., 73
Corporate victimization, 10
Correctional institutions, 10
Crime rates: and density, 47-53, 80; and urban structural characteristics, 90-93
Crimes, classification of, 37-43, 79-80
Crimes, reporting of, 21-22, 23-24, 65, 73
Criminal-justice system, 6-8, 11, 17, 81
Criminal law, 3, 4, 10
Criminal Prisons of London, The (Mayhew and Binny), 14
Critical-intensity zones, 56, 61, 77-78
Crowding (internal density), 45-53 *passim*, 60, 80
Cunningham, C.L., 70, 74, 77-78
Curtis, L.A., 56, 71

Dadrian, V.N., 1
Dallas, 19, 35
Data, 21-35; aggregate-level, 18; validity of, 79; victimization data vs. crime data, 57. *See also* National Crime Surveys; Uniform Crime Reports
Decker, S.H., 24, 34, 55, 73
Denno, D., and Cramer, J.A., 6
Density, defined, 46
Denver, 19, 35
Detroit, 15, 19
Diamond, A.S., 3
Dynes, R.R., and Quarantelli, E.L., 9-10

"Ecological Correlations and the Behavior of Individuals" (Robinson), 16
Ecological studies of crime, 13-18, 20
Edwards, C., 3
Elderly, victimization of, 10, 65, 73-78
Ellenberger, Henri, 5
Elmer, M.C., 13
Empey, L.T., 65
England, 13-14
Ennis, P.H., 25, 35 n.3

Environmental control indicators (police per capita/population density), 55
Expenditure and Employment Data for the Criminal Justice System (U.S. Justice Dept.), 62
External density. *See* Population density

Faris, R.E.L., 14
Fattah, E.A., 5
Fear of victimization, 73-74
Federal Bureau of Investigation (FBI), 21, 27
Feyerherm, W.H., and Hindelang, M.J., 65
Finestone, H., 15
Firefighters as victims, 9
Fletcher, J., 14
Fooner, M., 22
Foreign-born population, percentage of: and juvenile victimization, 68, 70, 71
France, 13, 45
Freedman, J., Heska, S., and Levy, A., 48
Friedman, C.J., Mann, F., and Adelman, H., 65
Furstenberg, F.F., 10

Galaway, B., and Hudson, J., 5-6, 8
Galle, O., Gove, W.R., and McPherson, J.M., 47
Galle, O., McCarthy, J.D., and Gove, W.R., 48
Garabedian, P.G., 37
Geis, G., 8
Georges, D.E., and Harries, K.D., 17
Gibbons, D.C., 37
Glaser, B.G., and Strauss, A.L., 37
Glaser, D., 37
Glyde, John, 14
Goldsmith, J., and Goldsmith, S.S., 10, 65
Goldstein, 22
Gordon, R.A., 16, 61
Gove, W.R., and Hughes, M., 47, 49
Gove, W.R., Hughes, M., and Galle, O., 52

Greenwood, M.J., and Wadycki, W.J., 22, 49, 57
Gross-density measures, 46-47
Guardians, 53
Gubrium, J.F., 73
Guerry, A.M., 13, 45

Hage, J., 37, 56
Hammurabi, code of, 3
Harland, A.T., 8
Harries, K.D., 17, 41, 48, 56, 57
Harries, K.D., and Brunn, S.D., 17
Hawley, A.H., 20
Hemley, D.D., and McPheters, L.R., 45, 59
Hendricks, J., and Hendricks, C.D., 74
Hepburn, R., and Monti, D.J., 65
Herbert, D., 17
Hindelang, M.J., 17-18
Homicide, 48
Hood, R., and Sparks, R., 23
Household crimes, 73-78, 86
Houston, 15-16, 19
Human ecology: and crime, 13-18, 20

Impact Cities Program (LEAA), 23
In-dwelling density, 47
Income level, 74
Indianapolis, 15
"Indices to moral influences/moral results" (Fletcher), 14
Internal density. See Crowding
International Association of Chiefs of Police (IACP), 21

Jacobs, J., 56
Jeffrey, C.R., 55
Jonassen, C.T., 16
Juvenile delinquency, 15
Juvenile victimization, 65-72

Kansas City, 74
Kingship, 4
Kirmeyer, S.L., 46, 47
Knudten, M.S., and Knudten, R.D., 7
Kvalseth, T.O., 28, 46, 72 n.4, 77

Labowitz, B.D., 73
Lalli, M., and Savitz, L.D., 65
Lamborn, L.L., 8, 10
Lander, B., 15
Larceny: defined, 85, 87; and elderly victimization, 74, 75, 77, 78; household, 38, 49, 50, 52, 63, 85; and juvenile victimization, 67, 68, 70, 71; personal, 32, 33, 34, 38, 40, 49, 50, 52, 60, 85; and police per capita, 63
Laster, R.E., 3
Law Enforcement Assistance Administration, 23, 27, 35, 55, 73
Lazarsfeld, P.F., 37
LEAA. See Law Enforcement Assistance Administration
Levin, Y., and Lindesmith, A., 14
Levine, J.P., 22, 23, 24
Lindsey, D.B., 10
"Localities of Crimes in Suffolk" (Glyde), 14
Lorenz, K., 56
Los Angeles, 19

McCarthy, J.D., Galle, O.R., and Zimmern, W., 46, 48
McDonald, W.F., 10
McKinney, J.C., 37
Maine, H.S., 3
Maltz, M.D., 22, 35
Mayhew, B.H., and Levinger, R.L., 45, 57, 59, 60
Mayhew, H., 14
Meiners, R.E., 3
Mendelsohn, Benjamin, 1, 4, 37
Methodology, 18-19
Miami, 19
Milakovich, M.E., and Weis, K., 22
Miller, W.B., 28
Milwaukee, 19
Minneapolis, 19
Mladenka, K.R., and Hill, K.Q., 45, 70
Morris, T., 14, 45
Motor-vehicle theft, 24, 25, 30, 32-33, 34, 49, 51, 52, 67, 68, 71, 79, 85, 87

Multiple regression, stepwise, 66-67, 75-76
Mutual victimization, 5

National Crime Panel Surveys (NCPS), 35
National Crime Surveys, 17, 19, 49, 57, 79; and classification of victimization, 37-43 *passim*; compared with Uniform Crime Reports, 23-35; survey design, 83-84; and urban structural characteristics, 90-93
National Opinion Research Center (NORC), 23, 25
National Organization of Victim Assistance (NOVA), 1
NCS. *See* National Crime Surveys
Nelson, J.F., 24, 34, 55
Nettler, G., 13
Newark, 19, 35
Newman, D.J., 6
Newman, O., 42
New Orleans, 19
New York, 19
Nomological validation, 26-27, 28, 30-32, 33, 34
Nonproperty assaultive crimes, 38-42 *passim*; and juvenile victimization, 66-72; and police per capita/population density, 58-62, 81. *See also* Assault, simple/aggravated
Normandeau, A., 5

Oakland, 19
Organizations as victims, 9-10

Pathology: and crowding, 48
Pecar, J., 10
Penick, K.K.E., and Owens, M.E.B., III, 23, 32, 35
Perceived density, 52
Personal crimes, 65, 86
Philadelphia, 19
Piazza, T., 41
Piliavin, I., and Briar, S., 22
Pittsburgh, 19
Pokorny, A., 22

Police: and reporting of crime, 22; as victims, 9-10; victimization by, 10
Police decision making: victim's role in, 8
Police per capita: and criminal victimization, 55-63, 81
Political victims, 6
Poor Pay More, The (Caplovitz), 9
Pope, C.E., 17
Population between 12 and 19 years of age, percentage of: and juvenile victimization, 69, 72
Population density, 38, 40, 41, 42, 80, 81; and criminal victimization, 45-53; and elderly victimization, 75-78; and juvenile victimization, 66-72; and police per capita (as environmental indicators), 55-63
Portland, 19, 35
Precipitative victims, 6
President's Commission on Law Enforcement and Administration of Justice, 23, 55-56
Pressman, I., and Carol, A., 48
Primary victimization, 5
Pritchard, J.B., 6
Property-crime index, 80
Property crimes: and classification of criminal victimization, 38-43; and juvenile victimization, 66-71; and police per capita/population density, 58-62, 81; with/without contact, 48-53 *passim*
Provocative victims, 6
Public assistance, percentage of population on: and elderly victimization, 76, 78
Public education, 7

Quetelet, L.A.J., 13
Quinney, R., 16

Rape, 25, 32, 33, 34, 38, 41, 48-49, 50; defined, 86, 87; and juvenile victimization, 68, 69, 71
Rapoport, A., 47
Rawson, R.W., 13-14

Reckless, W.C., 4-5
Reppetto, T.A., 16-17, 28, 42, 59-60, 61, 70, 74, 78
Residential crowding concept, 47
Restitution programs, 7, 8
Retail stores as victims, 9-10
Retributive justice, 3
Reverse-record checks, 23, 32
Robbery, 30, 32, 33, 34, 38, 40, 41, 42, 79; defined, 86, 87; personal, 48, 49-50, 52
Robinson, W.S., 16
Roebuck, J.B., 37
Roman Catholic Church, 4
Roman law, 3
Roncek, D.W., 18, 49
Rosen, L., and Turner, S.H., 16
Rosenblum, R.H., and Blew, C.H., 7
Rubenstein, J., 22

Saint Louis, 16, 19, 35
Sample, 80-81, 83
San Diego, 19
San Francisco, 19
Schafer, S., 2, 3, 4
Schmidt, C.F., 15
Schmidt, D.E., Goldman, R.P., and Flimer, N.R., 46
Schneider, A.L., and Schneider, P.S., 8
Schrag, C., 37
Schuessler, K., 16
Seattle, 15
SEC. See Socioeconomic indexes
Secondary victimization, 5
SEI. See Socioeconomic indexes
Seidman, D., and Couzens, M., 22
Self-victimizing victims, 6
Sellin, T., and Wolfgang, M.E., 5, 8, 70
Selltiz, C., Wrightsman, L.S., and Cook, S., 26
Sengstock, M.C., and Liang, J., 10
Sex ratio, 74
Shaw, C.R., and McKay, H.D., 14-15, 18, 28, 45, 49, 59, 65, 70
Sheleff, L.S., 10

Sheleff, L.S., and Shichor, D., 10
Shichor, D., 10
Shichor, D., Decker, D.L., and O'Brien, R.M., 17, 28, 72
Skogan, W.G., 17, 18, 22, 23, 24, 34, 45, 49, 55, 57, 59
Slatin, G.I., 18, 49
Smigel, E.O., and Ross, H.L., 9
Socially weak victims, 6
Socioeconomic indexes: and elderly victimization, 75, 76, 77, 78; and juvenile victimization, 66, 68, 70, 72
Spector, P.E., 48
Suicide, 48
Sundeen, R.A., and Mathieu, J.T., 73
Sutherland, E.H., and Cressey, D.R., 18
Swimmer, G., 57
Sykes, G.M., 37

Tacitus, 3
Task Force Report: Crime and Its Impact, 15
Telescoping (of crime reports), 23, 35
Television, influence of, 74
Tertiary victimization, 3
Tittle, C.R., Willemer, W.J., and Smith, D.A., 28
Torts, law of (civil law), 3

UCR. See Uniform Crime Reports
Unemployment: and juvenile victimization, 68-69
Uniform Crime Reports, 16, 17, 49, 79; and classification of victimization, 40, 41, 42; compared with National Crime Surveys, 21-35; definitions, 86-87; and urban structural characteristics, 90-93
U.S. Bureau of the Census, 23, 27, 35, 47, 49, 57, 73, 75; 1970 Census of Population and Housing, 83
U.S. Department of Health, Education and Welfare, 65
U.S. Department of Justice, 26, 27, 37, 57, 60, 62, 71, 73, 74, 84
U.S. House of Representatives, 73

University of Chicago, 14, 65
Unrelated victims, 6
Urban structural characteristics, 18-19, 27-28; and classification of victimization, 37-43 *passim*; and elderly victimization, 75-78; and juvenile victimization, 66-72; and NCS/UCR rates, 90-93

Validity assessment, 25-27, 79
Van den Berghe, P.L., 56, 60
Victim-assistance programs, 6-8, 11
Victim characteristics: and offender conviction, 6, 8
Victim classifications, 4-6
Victim compensation/restitution, 3, 7-8, 11
Victim counseling, 7
Victim-criminal contact, 38-43
Victim, and criminal justice system, 6-8, 11
Victim-criminal relationship, 6, 10-11
Victim, defined, 1-2
Victim, family and friends of, 12
Victim individualization, 8
Victim as offender, 12
Victim proneness, 11
"Victim public," 10
Victim recidivism, 11
Victim responsibility for the crime, 5-6
Victim, role of: and police decision making, 8
Victim, role of: and reporting of crimes, 21
Victim, status of, in the past, 2-4
Victim targets, 10
Victimity, 1, 9
Victimization: classification of, 37-43; in correctional institutions, 10; differential impact of, 74; of elderly, 65, 73-78; fear of, 73-74; of juveniles, 65-72; of organizations, 9-10; and police per capita, 55-63;

and population density/crowding, 45-53; typology of, 5
Victimization studies, 10-12
Victimization surveys, 21-35
Victimogenesis, 5
Victimology, 1, 4
Victimology (journal), 1
Violent crimes, 40-42, 48, 49, 65
Von Hentig, H., 4, 5, 37
Voss, H.L., and Petersen, D.M., 13, 15

Wales, 13-14
Walker, N., 22
Washington, D.C., 19, 35
Weathersby, G.B., 57
White population, percentage of: and juvenile victimization, 67-68, 70, 71
Wilks, J.A., 15
Williams, K.M., 6
Wilson, J.Q., 22, 45, 66
Wilson, J.Q., and Boland, B., 45, 48, 53, 59, 70
Winch, R.F., 37
Wirth, L., 17, 18, 28, 45, 46, 49, 59, 70
Witness services, 7
Wolfgang, M.E., 5, 8, 45, 59, 70, 71
Wolfgang, M.E., Figlio, R.M., and Sellin, T., 12
Wolfgang, M.E., and Ferracuti, F., 22, 56
Wolfgang, M.E., and Singer, S.I., 10-12, 23, 37
Women, 74
Wood, A.L., 37
World Society of Victimology, 1
Wrongfully accused person, 10

Young Rifai, M.A., 10, 73, 74

Zellitz, Wrightsman, and Cook, 26
Ziegenhagen, E.A., 1, 2

About the Authors

David L. Decker is professor and chair of the Department of Sociology at California State College, San Bernardino. He is the author of *Social Gerontology: An Introduction to the Dynamics of Aging* and has published articles in the areas of social theory, social gerontology, and criminal victimization.

David Shichor received the B.A. from Hebrew University in 1962; the M.A. from California State College, Los Angeles, in 1966; and the Ph.D. from the University of Southern California in 1970. He is currently associate professor of sociology at California State College, San Bernardino. Professor Shichor is the coeditor (with Delos H. Kelly) of *Critical Issues in Juvenile Delinquency* (Lexington Books 1980) and has published more than thirty articles and chapters, mainly in the fields of juvenile delinquency, criminology, and victimology. His most recent articles have appeared in *Criminology, The British Journal of Criminology, Journal of Criminal Justice, Deviant Behavior, Sociological Quarterly, Criminal Justice Review, Crime and Delinquency,* and *The Gerontologist.*

Robert M. O'Brien is associate professor of sociology at the University of Oregon. His recent articles have appeared in the *American Sociological Review, American Journal of Political Science, Criminology, Journal of Criminal Justice, Political Behavior, Social Forces,* and *Sociological Quarterly.* His major research interests focus on the areas of statistical methodology (especially measurement problems) and the ecological correlates of crime and victimization rates.